33031

W9-CZT-877

Their Wedding Journey

Their
Wedding Journey

By

William D. Howells

Toronto:

The Musson Book Co., Limited

MUSSON
ALL CANADIAN PRODUCTION

CONTENTS

Their Wedding Journey

I.

T HEY first met in Boston, but the match was made in Europe, where they afterwards saw each other; whither, indeed, he followed her; and there the match was also broken off. Why it was broken off, and why it was renewed after a lapse of years, is part of quite a long love-story, which I do not think myself qualified to rehearse, distrusting my fitness for a sustained or involved narration; though I am persuaded that a skilful romancer could turn the courtship of Basil and Isabel March to excellent account. Fortunately for me, however, in attempting to tell the reader of the wedding-journey of a newly married couple, no longer very young, to be sure, but still fresh in the light of their love, I shall have nothing to do but to talk of some ordinary traits of American life as these appeared to them, to speak a little of well-known and easily accessible places, to present now a bit of landscape and now a sketch of character.

They had agreed to make their wedding-journey in the simplest and quietest way, and as it did not take place at once after their marriage, but some weeks later, it had all the desired charm of privacy from the outset.

"How much better," said Isabel, "to go now, when nobody cares whether you go or stay, than to have started off upon a wretched wedding-breakfast all tears and trousseau, and had people wanting to see you aboard the cars. Now there will not be a suspicion of honey-moon-shine about us; we shall go just like anybody else,—with a difference, dear, with a difference!" and she took Basil's cheeks between her hands. In order to do this, she had to run round the table; for they were at dinner, and Isabel's aunt, with whom they had begun married life, sat substantial between them. It was rather a girlish thing for Isabel, and she added, with a conscious blush, "We are past our first youth, you know; and we shall not strike the public as bridal, shall we? My one horror in life is an evident bride."

Basil looked at her fondly, as if he did not think her at all too old to be taken for a bride; and for my part I do not object to a woman's being of Isabel's age, if she is of a good heart and temper. Life must have been very unkind to her if at that age she have not won more than she has lost. It seemed to Basil that his wife was quite as fair as when they met first, eight years before; but he could not help recurring with an inextinguishable regret to the long interval of their broken engagement, which but for that fatality they might have spent together, he imagined, in just such rapture as this. The regret always haunted him, more or less; it was part of his love; the loss accounted irreparable really enriched the final gain.

"I don't know," he said presently, with as much gravity as a man can whose cheeks are clasped between a lady's hands, "you don't begin very well for a bride who wishes to keep her secret. If you behave in this way, they will put us into the 'bridal chambers' at all the hotels. And the cars—they're beginning to have them on the palace-cars."

Just then a shadow fell into the room.

"Wasn't that thunder, Isabel?" asked her aunt, who had been contentedly surveying the tender spectacle before her. "O dear! you'll never be able to go by the boat to-night if it storms. It's actually raining now!"

In fact, it was the beginning of that terrible storm of June, 1870. All in a moment, out of the hot sunshine of the day it burst upon us before we quite knew that it threatened, even before we had fairly noticed the clouds, and it went on from passion to passion with an inexhaustible violence. In the square upon which our friends looked out of their dining-room windows the trees whitened in the gusts, and darkened in the driving floods of the rainfall, and in some paroxysms of the tempest bent themselves in desperate submission, and then with a great shudder rent away whole branches and flung them far off upon the ground. Hail mingled with the rain, and now the few umbrellas that had braved the storm vanished, and the hurtling ice crackled upon the pavement, where the lightning played like flames burning from the earth, while the thunder roared overhead without ceasing. There was something splendidly theatrical about it all; and when a street-car, laden to the last inch of its capacity, came by, with horses that pranced and leaped under the stinging blows of the hail-stones, our friends felt as if it were an effective and very naturalistic bit of pantomime contrived for their admiration. Yet as to themselves they were very sensible of a potent reality in the affair, and at intervals during the storm they debated about going at all that day, and decided to go and not to go, according to the changing complexion of the elements. Basil had said that as this was their first journey together in America, he wished to give it at the beginning as pungent a national character as possible, and that as he could imagine nothing more peculiarly American than a voyage to New York by a Fall River boat, they ought to take that route thither. So much upholstery, so much music, such variety of company, he understood, could not be got in any other way, and it might be that they would even catch a glimpse of the inventor of the combination, who represented the very excess and extremity of a certain kind of Americanism. Isabel had eagerly consented; but these æsthetic motives were paralyzed for her by the thought of passing Point Judith in a storm, and she descended from her high intents first to the Inside Boats, without the magnificence and the orchestra, and then to the idea of going by land in a sleeping-car. Having comfortably accomplished this feat, she treated Basil's consent as a matter of course, not because she did not regard him, but because as a woman she could not conceive of the steps to her conclusion as unknown to him, and always treated her own decisions as the product of their common reasoning. But her husband held out for the boat, and insisted that if the storm fell before seven o'clock, they could reach it at Newport by the last express; and it was this obstinacy that, in proof of Isabel's wisdom, obliged them to wait two hours in the station before going by the land route. The storm abated at five o'clock, and though the rain continued, it seemed well by a quarter of seven to set out for the Old Colony Depot, in sight of which a sudden and vivid flash of lightning caused Isabel to seize her husband's arm, and to implore him, "O don't go by the boat!" On this, Basil had the incredible weakness to yield; and bade the driver take them to the Worcester Depot. It was the first swerving from the ideal in their wedding journey, but it was by no means the last; though it must be confessed that it was early to begin.

They both felt more tranquil when they were irretrievably committed by the purchase of their tickets, and when they sat down in the waiting-room of the station, with all the time between seven and nine o'clock before them. Basil would have eked out the business of checking the trunks into an affair of some length, but the baggagemaster did his duty with pitiless celerity; and so Basil, in the mere excess of his disoccupation, bought an accident-insurance ticket. This employed him half a minute, and then he gave up the unequal contest, and went and took his place beside Isabel, who sat prettily wrapped in her shawl, perfectly content.

"Isn't it charming," she said gaily, "having to wait so long? It puts me in mind of some of those other journeys we took together. But I can't think of those times with any patience, when we might really have had each other, and didn't! Do you remember how long we had to wait at Chambéry? and the numbers of military gentlemen that waited too, with their little waists, and their kisses when they met? and that poor married military gentleman with the plain wife and the two children, and a tarnished uniform? He seemed to be somehow in misfortune, and his moustache hung down in such a spirit-less way, while all the other military moustaches about curled and bristled with so much boldness. I think *salles d'attente* everywhere are delightful; and there is such a community of interest in them all, that when I come here only to go out to Brookline, I feel myself a traveller once more,—a blessed stranger in a strange land. O dear, Basil, those were happy times after all, when we might have had each other and didn't! And now we're the more precious for having been so long lost."

She drew closer and closer to him, and looked at him in a way that threatened betrayal of her bridal charac-ter.

"Isabel, you will be having your head on my shoulder, next," said he.

"Never!" she answered fiercely, recovering her dist-ance with a start. "But, dearest, if you do see me going to—act absurdly, you know, do stop me."

"I'm very sorry, but I've got myself to stop. Besides, I didn't undertake to preserve the *incognito* of this bridal party."

If any accident of the sort dreaded had really hap-pened, it would not have mattered so much, for as yet they were the sole occupants of the waiting-room. To be sure, the ticket-seller was there, and the lady who checked packages left in her charge; but these must have seen so many endearments pass between passengers, that a fleeting caress or two would scarcely have drawn their notice to our pair. Yet Isabel did not so much even as put her hand into her husband's; and as Basil after-wards said, it was very good practice.

Our temporary state, whatever it is, is often mirrored

in all that come near us, and our friends were fated to meet frequent parodies of their happiness from first to last on this journey. The travesty began with the very first people who entered the waiting-room after themselves, and who were a very young couple starting like themselves upon a pleasure tour, which also was evidently one of the first tours of any kind that they had made. It was of modest extent, and comprised going to New York and back; but they talked of it with a fluttered and joyful expectation as if it were a voyage to Europe. Presently there appeared a burlesque of their happiness (but with a touch of tragedy) in that kind of young man who is called by the females of his class a fellow, and two young women of that kind known to him as girls. He took a place between these, and presently began a robust flirtation with one of them. He possessed himself, after a brief struggle, of her parasol, and twirled it about, as he uttered, with a sort of tender rudeness, inconceivable vapidities, such as you would expect from none but a man of the highest fashion. The girl thus courted became selfishly unconscious of everything but her own joy, and made no attempt to bring the other girl within its warmth, but left her to languish forgotten on the other side. The latter sometimes leaned forward, and tried to divert a little of the flirtation to herself, but the flirters snubbed her with short answers, and presently she gave up and sat still in the sad patience of uncourted women. In this attitude she became a burden to Isabel, who was glad when the three took themselves away, and were succeeded by a very stylish couple—from New York, she knew as well as if they had given her their address on West 999th Street. The lady was not pretty,

B

and she was not, Isabel thought, dressed in the perfect
taste of Boston; but she owned frankly to herself that
the New Yorkeress was stylish, undeniably effective. The
gentleman bought a ticket for New York, and remained
at the window of the office talking quite easily with the
seller.

"You couldn't do that, my poor Basil," said Isabel,
"you'd be afraid."

"O dear, yes; I'm only too glad to get off without
browbeating; though I must say that this officer looks
affable enough. Really," he added, as an acquaintance
of the ticket-seller came in and nodded to him and said,
'Hot, to-day!' "this is very strange. I always felt as if
these men had no private life, no friendships like the
rest of us. On duty they seem so like sovereigns, set
apart from mankind, and above us all, that it's quite incredible they should have the common personal rela-
tions."

At intervals of their talk and silence there came vivid
flashes of lightning and quite heavy shocks of thunder,
very consoling to our friends, who took them as so many
compliments to their prudence in not going by the boat,
and who had secret doubts of their wisdom whenever
these acknowledgments were withheld. Isabel went so far
as to say that she hoped nothing would happen to the
boat, but I think she would cheerfully have learnt that
the vessel had been obliged to put back to Newport, on
account of the storm, or even that it had been driven
ashore at a perfectly safe place.

People constantly came and went in the waiting-room,
which was sometimes quite full, and again empty of all
but themselves. In the course of their observations they

formed many cordial friendships and bitter enmities upon the ground of personal appearance, or particulars of dress, with people whom they saw for half a minute upon an average; and they took such a keen interest in every one, that it would be hard to say whether they were more concerned in an old gentleman with vigorously upright iron-grey hair, who sat fronting them, and reading all the evening papers, or a young man who hurled himself through the door, bought a ticket with terrific precipitation, burst out again, and then ran down a departing train before it got out of the station; they loved the old gentleman for a certain stubborn benevolence of expression, and if they had been friends of the young man and his family for generations, and felt bound if any harm befell him to go and break the news gently to his parents, their nerves could not have been more intimately wrought upon by his hazardous behaviour. Still, as they had their tickets for New York, and he was going out on a merely local train,—to Brookline, I believe,—they could not, even in their anxiety, repress a feeling of contempt for his unambitious destination.

They were already as completely cut off from local associations and sympathies as if they were a thousand miles and many months away from Boston. They enjoyed the lonely flaring of the gas-jets as a gust of wind drew through the station; they shared the gloom and isolation of a man who took a seat in the darkest corner of the room, and sat there with folded arms, the genius of absence. In the patronizing spirit of travellers in a foreign country they noted and approved the vases of cut-flowers in the booth of the lady who checked packages, and the pots of ivy in her windows. "These poor Bostonians," they said, "have some love of the beautiful in their rugged natures."

But after all was said and thought, it was only eight o'clock, and they still had an hour to wait.

Basil grew restless, and Isabel said, with a subtle interpretation of his uneasiness, "*I* don't want anything to eat, Basil, but I think I know the weaknesses of men; and you had better go and pass the next half-hour over a plate of something indigestible."

This was said *con stizza*, the least little suggestion of it; but Basil rose with shameful alacrity. "Darling, if it's your wish"—

"It's my fate, Basil," said Isabel.

—"I'll go," he exclaimed, "because it isn't bridal, and will help us to pass for old married people."

"No, no, Basil, be honest; fibbing isn't your *forte*: I wonder you went into the insurance business; you ought to have been a lawyer. Go because you like eating, and are hungry, perhaps, or think you may be so before we get to New York. I shall amuse myself well enough here."

I suppose it is always a little shocking and grievous to a wife when she recognizes a rival in butchers'-meat and the vegetables of the season. With her slender relishes for pastry and confectionery, and her dainty habits of lunching, she cannot reconcile with the ideal her husband's capacity for breakfasting, dining, supping, and hot meals at all hours of the day and night—as they write it on the sign-boards of barbaric eating-houses. But Isabel would have only herself to blame if she had not perceived this trait of Basil's before marriage. She recurred now, as his figure disappeared down the station, to memorable instances of his appetite in their European travels during their first engagement. "Yes, he ate terribly at Susa, when I was too full of the notion of getting into Italy to care for *bouillon* and cold roast chicken. At Rome I thought I must break with him on account of the wild-boar; and at Heidelberg, the sausage and the ham!—how could he, in my presence? But I took him with all his faults,—and was glad to get him," she added, ending her meditation with a little burst of candour; and she did not even think of Basil's appetite when he reappeared.

With the thronging of many sorts of people, in parties and singly, into the waiting room, they became once again mere observers of their kind, more or less critical in temper, until the crowd grew so that individual traits were merged in the character of multitude. Even then, they could catch glimpses of faces so sweet or fine that they made themselves felt like moments of repose in the tumult, and here and there was something so grotesque in dress or manner that it showed distinct from the rest. The ticket-seller's stamp clicked incessantly as he sold tickets to all points South and West: to New York, Philadelphia, Charleston; to New Orleans, Chicago, Omaha; to St. Paul, Duluth, St. Louis; and it would not have been hard to find in that anxious bustle, that unsmiling eagerness, an image of the whole busy affair of life. It was not a particularly sane spectacle, that impatience to be off to some place that lay not only in the distance, but also in the future—to which no line of road carries you with absolute certainty across an interval of time full of every imaginable chance and influence. It is easy enough to buy a ticket to Cincinnati, but it is somewhat harder to arrive there. Say that all goes well, is it exactly *you* who arrive?

In the midst of the disquiet there entered at last an old woman, so very infirm that she had to be upheld on either hand by her husband and the hackman who had brought them, while a young girl went before with shawls and pillows which she arranged upon the seat. There the invalid lay down, and turned towards the crowd a white, suffering face, which was yet so heavenly meek and peaceful that it comforted whoever looked at it. In spirit our happy friends bowed themselves before it and owned that there was something better than happiness in it.

"What is it like, Isabel?"

"O, I don't know, darling," she said; but she thought, "Perhaps it is like some blessed sorrow that takes us out of this prison of a world, and sets us free of our every-day hates and desires, our aims, our fears, ourselves. Maybe a long and mortal sickness might come to wear such a face in one of us two, and the other could see it, and not regret the poor mask of youth and pretty looks that had fallen away."

She rose and went over to the sick woman, on whose face beamed a tender smile, as Isabel spoke to her. A chord thrilled in two lives hitherto unknown to each other; but what was said Basil would not ask when the invalid had taken Isabel's hand between her own, as for adieu, and she came back to his side with swimming eyes. Perhaps his wife could have given no good reason for her emotion, if he had asked it. But it made her very sweet and dear to him; and I suppose that when a tolerably unselfish man is once secure of a woman's love, he is ordinarily more affected by her compassion and tenderness for other objects than by her feelings towards himself. He likes well enough to think, "She loves me," but still better, "How kind and good she is!"

They lost sight of the invalid in the hurry of getting places on the cars, and they never saw her again. The man at the wicket-gate leading to the train had thrown it up, and the people were pressing furiously through as if their lives hung upon the chance of instant passage. Basil had secured his ticket for the sleeping-car, and so he and Isabel stood aside and watched the tumult. When the rush was over they passed through, and as they walked up and down the platform beside the train, "I was thinking," said Isabel, "after I spoke to that poor old lady, of what Clara Williams says: that she wonders the happiest women in the world can look each other in the face without bursting into tears, their happiness is so unreasonable, and so built upon and hedged about with misery. She declares that there's nothing so sad to her as a bride, unless it's a young mother, or a little girl growing up in the innocent gaiety of her heart. She wonders they can live through it."

"Clara is very much of a reformer, and would make an end of all of us men, I suppose,—except her father, who supports her in the leisure that enables her to do her deep thinking. She little knows what we poor fellows have to suffer, and how often we break down in business hours, and sob upon one another's necks. Did that old lady talk to you in the same strain?"

"O no! she spoke very calmly of her sickness, and said she had lived a blessed life. Perhaps it was that made me shed those few small tears. She seemed a very religious person."

"Yes," said Basil, "it is almost a pity that religion is going out. But then you are to have the franchise."

"All aboard!"

This warning cry saved him from whatever heresy he might have been about to utter; and presently the train carried them out into the gas-sprinkled darkness, with an ever-growing speed that soon left the city lamps far behind. It is a phenomenon whose commonness alone prevents it from being most impressive, that departure of the night-express. The two hundred miles it is to travel stretch before it, traced by those slender clews, to lose which is ruin, and about which hang so many dangers. The draw-bridges that gape upon the way, the trains that stand smoking and steaming on the track, the rail that has borne the wear so long that it must soon snap under it, the deep cut where the overhanging mass of rock trembles to its fall, the obstruction that a pitiless malice may have placed in your path,—you think of these after the journey is done, but they seldom haunt your fancy while it lasts. The knowledge of your helplessness in any circumstances is so perfect that it begets a sense of irresponsibility, almost of security; and as you drowse upon the pallet of the sleeping-car, and feel youreslf hurled forward through the obscurity, you are almost thankful that you can do nothing, for it is upon this condition only that you can endure it; and some such condition as this, I suppose, accounts for many heroic facts in the world. To the fantastic mood which possesses you equally, sleeping or waking, the stoppages of the train have a weird character; and Worcester, Springfield,

New Haven, and Stamford are rather points in dream-
land than well-known towns of New England. As the
train stops you drowse if you have been waking, and
wake if you have been in a doze; but in any case you are
aware of the locomotive hissing and coughing beyond the
station, of flaring gas-jets, of clattering feet of passengers getting on and off; then of some one, conductor or
station-master, walking the whole length of the train;
and then you are aware of an insane satisfaction in renewed flight through the darkness. You think hazily of
the folk in their beds in the town left behind, who stir
uneasily at the sound of your train's departing whistle;
and so all is a blank vigil or a blank slumber.

By daylight Basil and Isabel found themselves at opposite ends of the car, struggling severally with the problem of the morning's toilet. When the combat was ended,
they were surprised at the decency of their appearance,
and Isabel said, "I think I'm presentable to an early
Broadway public, and I've a fancy for not going to a
hotel. Lucy will be expecting us out there before noon;
and we can pass the time pleasantly enough for a few
hours just wandering about." She was a woman who
loved any cheap defiance of custom, and she had an
agreeable sense of adventure in what she proposed. Besides, she felt that nothing could be more in the uncon-
ventional spirit in which they meant to make their whole
journey than a stroll about New York at half-past six
in the morning.

"Delightful!" answered Basil, who was always
charmed with these small originalities. "You look well
enough for an evening party; and besides, you won't
meet one of your own critical class on Broadway at this

hour. We will breakfast at one of those gilded metro-
politan restaurants, and then go round to Leonard's,
who will be able to give us just three unhurried seconds.
After that we'll push on out to his place."

At that early hour there were not many people astir
on the wide avenue down which our friends strolled
when they left the station; but in the aspect of those they
saw there was something that told of a greater heat than
they had yet known in Boston, and they were sensible
of having reached a more southern latitude. The air,
though freshened by the over-night's storm, still wanted
the briskness and sparkle and pungency of the Boston
air, which is as delicious in summer as it is terrible in
winter; and the faces that showed themselves were
sodden from the yesterday's heat and perspiration. A
corner-grocer, seated in a sort of fierce despondency
upon a keg near his shop door, had lightly equipped himself for the struggle of the day in the battered armour
of the day before, and in a pair of roomy pantaloons, and
a baggy shirt of neutral tint,—perhaps he had made a
vow not to change it whilst the siege of the hot weather
lasted,—now confronted the advancing sunlight, before
which the long shadows of the buildings were slowly re-
tiring. A marketing mother of a family paused at a
provision-store, and looking weakly in at the white-
aproned butcher among his meats and flies, passed without an effort to purchase. Hurried and wearied shop-
girls tripped by in the draperies that betrayed their sad
necessity to be both fine and shabby; from a boarding-
house door issued briskly one of those cool young New
Yorkers whom no circumstances can oppress: breezy-
coated, white-linened, clean, with a good cigar in the

mouth, a light cane caught upon the elbow of one of the arms holding up the paper from which the morning's news is snatched, whilst the person sways lightly with the walk; in the street-cars that slowly tinkled up and down were rows of people with baskets between their legs and papers before their faces; and all showed by some peculiarity of air or dress the excess of heat which they had already borne, and to which they seemed to look forward, and gave by the scantiness of their number a vivid impression of the uncounted thousands within doors prolonging, before the day's terror began, the oblivion of sleep.

As they turned into one of the numerical streets to cross to Broadway, and found themselves in a yet deeper seclusion, Basil began to utter in a musing tone:—

> "A city against the world's grey Prime,
> Lost in some desert, far from Time,
> Where noiseless Ages gliding through
> Have only sifted sands and dew,—
> Yet still a marble hand of man
> Lying on all the haunted plan;
> The passions of the human heart
> Beating the marble breast of Art,—
> Were not more lone to one who first
> Upon its giant silence burst,
> Than this strange quiet, where the tide
> Of life, upheaved on either side,
> Hangs trembling, ready soon to beat
> With human waves the Morning Street."

"How lovely!" said Isabel, swiftly catching at her skirt, and deftly escaping contact with one of a long row of ash-barrels posted sentinel-like on the edge of the pavement. "Whose is it, Basil?"

"Ah! a poet's," answered her husband, "a man of whom we shall one day any of us be glad to say that we

liked him before he was famous. What a nebulous sweetness the first lines have, and what a clear, cool light of
day-break in the last!"

"You could have been as good a poet as that, Basil,"
said the ever-personal and concretely-speaking Isabel,
who could not look at a mountain without thinking what
Basil might have done in that way, if he had tried.

"O no, I couldn't, dear. It's very difficult being any
poet at all, though it's easy to be like one. But I've done
with it; I broke with the Muse the day you accepted me.
She came into my office, looking so shabby,—not unlike
one of those poor shop-girls; and as I was very well
dressed from having just been to see you, why, you
know, I felt the difference. 'Well, my dear?' said I,
not quite liking the look of reproach she was giving me.
'You are going to leave me,' she answered sadly. 'Well,
yes; I suppose I must. You see the insurance business
is very absorbing; and besides, it has a bad appearance,
you're coming about so in office hours, and in those
clothes.' 'O' she moaned out, 'you used to welcome me
at all times, out in the country, and thought me prettily
dressed.' 'Yes, yes; but this is Boston; and Boston makes
a great difference in one's ideas; and I'm going to be
married, too. Come, I don't want to seem ungrateful;
we *have* had many pleasant times together, I own it; and
I've no objections to your being present at Christmas
and Thanksgiving and birthdays, but really I must draw
the line there.' She gave me a look that made my heart
ache, and went straight to my desk and took out of a
pigeon-hole a lot of papers,—odes upon your cruelty,
Isabel; songs to you; sonnets,—the sonnet, a mighty poor
one, I'd made the day before,—and threw them all into

the grate. Then she turned to me again, signed adieu with mute lips, and passed out. I could hear the bottom wire of the poor thing's hoop-skirt clicking against each step of the stair-way, as she went slowly and heavily down to the street."

"O don't—*don't*, Basil," said his wife, "it seems like something wrong. I think you ought to have been ashamed."

"Ashamed! I was heart-broken. But it had to come to that. As I got hopeful about you, the Muse became a sad bore; and more than once I found myself smiling at her when her back was turned. The Muse doesn't like being laughed at any more than another woman would, and she would have left me shortly. No, I couldn't be a poet like our Morning Street friend. But see! the human wave is beginning to sprinkle the pavement with cooks and second-girls."

They were frowsy serving-maids and silent; each swept down her own door steps and the pavement in front of her own house, and then knocked her broom on the curb-stone and vanished into the house, on which the hand of change had already fallen. It was no longer a street solely devoted to the domestic gods, but had been invaded at more than one point by the bustling deities of business; in such streets the irregular, inspired doctors and doctresses come first with inordinate door-plates; then a milliner filling the parlour window with new bonnets; here even a publisher had hung his sign beside a door, through which the feet of young ladies used to trip, and the feet of little children to patter. Here and there stood groups of dwellings unmolested as yet outwardly; but even these had a certain careworn and guilty air, as if they knew themselves to be cheapish boarding-houses or furnished lodgings for gentlemen, and were trying to hide it. To these belonged the frowsy serving-women; to these the rows of ash-barrels, in which the decrepit children and mothers of the streets were clawing for bits of coal.

By the time Basil and Isabel reached Broadway there were already some omnibuses beginning their long day's travel up and down the handsome, tiresome length of that avenue; but for the most part it was empty. There was, of course, a hurry of foot-passengers upon the side-walks, but these were sparse and uncharacteristic, for New York proper was still fast asleep. The waiter at the restaurant into which our friends stepped was so well aware of this, and so perfectly assured they were not of the city, that he could not forbear a little patronage of them, which they did not resent. He brought Basil what he had ordered in barbaric abundance, and charged for it with barbaric splendour. It is all but impossible not to wish to stand well with your waiter: I have my-self been often treated with conspicuous rudeness by the tribe, yet I have never been able to withhold the *douceur* that marked me for a gentleman in their eyes, and entitled me to their dishonourable esteem. Basil was not superior to this folly, and left the waiter with the conviction that, if he was not a New Yorker, he was a high-bred man of the world at any rate.

Vexed by a sense of his own pitifulness, this man of the world continued his pilgrimage down Broadway, which even in that desert state was full of a certain interest. Troops of labourers straggled along the pavements, each with his dinner-pail in hand; and in many places the eternal building up and pulling down was already going on; carts were struggling up the slopes of vast cellars, with loads of distracting rubbish; here stood the half-demolished walls of a house, with a sad variety of wall-paper showing in the different rooms; there clinked the trowel upon the brick, yonder the hammer on the stone; overhead swung and threatened the marble block that the derrick was lifting to its place. As yet these forces of demolition and construction had the business of the street almost to themselves.

"Why, how shabby the street is!" said Isabel, at last. "When I landed, after being abroad, I remember that Broadway impressed me with its splendour."

"Ah! but you were merely coming from Europe then; and now you arrive from Boston, and are contrasting this poor Broadway with Washington Street. Don't be hard upon it, Isabel; every street can't be a Boston street, you know," said Basil. Isabel, herself a Bostonian of great intensity both by birth and conviction, believed her husband the only man able to have thoroughly baffled the malignity of the stars in causing him to be born out of Boston; yet he sometimes trifled with his hardly achieved triumph, and even showed an indifference to it, with an insincerity of which there can be no doubt whatever.

"O stuff!" she retorted, "as if I had any of that silly local pride! Though *you* know well enough that Boston *is* the best place in the world. But Basil! I suppose Broadway strikes us as so fine, on coming ashore from Europe, because we hardly expect anything of America then."

"Well, I don't know. Perhaps the street has some

positive grandeur of its own, though it needs a multitude of people in it to bring out its best effects. I'll allow its disheartening shabbiness and meanness in many ways; but to stand in front of Grace Church, on a clear day,— a day of late September, say,—and look down the swarming length of Broadway, on the movement and the numbers, while the Niagara roar swelled and swelled from those human rapids, was always like strong new wine to me. I don't think the world affords such another sight; and for one moment, at such times, I'd have been willing to be an Irish councilman, that I might have some right to the pride I felt in the capital of the Irish Republic. What a fine thing it must be for each victim of six centuries of oppression to reflect that he owns at least a dozen Americans, and that, with his fellows, he rules a hundred helpless millionaires!"

Like all daughters of a free country, Isabel knew nothing about politics, and she felt that she was getting into deep water; she answered buoyantly, but she was glad to make her weariness the occasion of hailing a stage, and changing the conversation. The further down town they went the busier the street grew; and about the Astor House, where they alighted, there was already a bustle that nothing but a fire could have created at the same hour in Boston. A little further on the steeple of Trinity rose high into the scorching sunlight, while below, in the shadow that was darker than it was cool, slumbered the old graves among their flowers.

"How still they lie!" mused the happy wife, peering through the iron fence in passing.

"Yes, their wedding-journeys are ended, poor things!" said Basil; and through both their minds flashed the wonder if they should ever come to something like that; but it appeared so impossible that they both smiled at the absurdity.

"It's too early yet for Leonard," continued Basil; "what a pity the churchyard is locked up! We could spend the time so delightfully in it. But, never mind; let us go down to the Battery,—it's not a very pleasant place, but it's near, and it's historical, and it's open,— where these drowsy friends of ours used to take the air when they were in the fashion, and had some occasion for the element in its freshness. You can imagine—it's cheap—how they used to see Mr. Burr and Mr. Hamilton down there."

All places that fashion has once loved and abandoned are very melancholy; but of all such places, I think the Battery is the most forlorn. Are there some sickly locust-trees there that cast a tremulous and decrepit shade upon the mangy grass-plots? I believe so, but I do not make sure; I am certain only of the mangy grass-plots, or rather the spaces between the paths, thinly over-grown with some kind of refuse and opprobrious weed, a stunted and pauper vegetation proper solely to the New York Battery. At that hour of the summer morning when our friends, with the aimlessness of strangers who are waiting to do something else, saw the ancient prom-enade, a few scant and hungry-eyed little boys and girls were wandering over this weedy growth, not playing, but moving listlessly to and fro, fantastic in the wild inaptness of their costumes. One of these little creatures wore, with an odd involuntary jauntiness, the cast-off best dress of some happier child, a gay little garment cut low in the neck and short in the sleeves, which gave

C

her the grotesque effect of having been at a party the
night before. Presently came two jaded women, a mother
and a grandmother, that appeared, when they had
crawled out of their beds, to have put on only so much
clothing as the law compelled. They abandoned themselves upon the green stuff, whatever it was, and, with
their lean hands clasped outside their knees, sat and
stared, silent and hopeless, at the eastern sky, at the
heart of the terrible furnace, into which in those days
the world seemed cast to be burnt up, while the child
which the younger woman had brought with her feebly
wailed unheeded at her side. On one side of these women
were the shameless houses out of which they might have
crept, and which somehow suggested riotous maritime
dissipation; on the other side were those houses in which
had once dwelt rich and famous folk, but which were
now dropping down the boarding-house scale through
various unhomelike occupations to final dishonour and
despair. Down nearer the water, and not far from the
castle that was once a playhouse and is now the depot
of emigration, stood certain express wagons, and about
these lounged a few hard-looking men. Beyond laughed
and danced the fresh blue water of the bay, dotted with
sails and smoke-stacks.

"Well," said Basil, "I think if I could choose, I should
like to be a friendless German boy, setting foot for the
first time on this happy continent. Fancy his rapture
on beholding this lovely spot, and these charming American faces! What a smiling aspect life in the New World
must wear to his young eyes, and how his heart must
leap within him!"

"Yes, Basil; it's all very pleasing, and thank you for

bringing me. But if you don't think of any other New York delights to show me, do let us go and sit in Leonard's office till he comes, and then get out into the country as soon as possible."

Basil defended himself against the imputation that he had been trying to show New York to his wife, or that he had any thought but of whiling away the long morning hours, until it should be time to go to Leonard. He protested that a knowledge of Europe made New York the most uninteresting town in America, and that it was the last place in the world where he should think of amusing himself or any one else; and then they both upbraided the city's bigness and dullness with an enjoyment that none but Bostonians can know. They particularly derided the notion of New York's being loved by anyone. It was immense, it was grand in some ways, parts of it were exceedingly handsome; but it was too vast, too coarse, too restless. They could imagine its being liked by a successful young man of business, or, by a rich young girl, ignorant of life and with not too nice a taste in her pleasures; but that it should be dear to any poet or scholar, or any woman of wisdom and refinement, that they could not imagine. They could not think of any one's loving New York as Dante loved Florence, or as Madame de Etaël loved Paris, or as Johnson loved black, homely, home-like London. And as they twittered their little dispraises, the giant Mother of Commerce was growing more and more conscious of herself, waking from her night's sleep and becoming aware of her fleets and trains, and the myriad hands and wheels that throughout the whole sea and land move for her, and do her will even while she sleeps. All about the wedding-journeyers

swelled the deep tide of life back from its night-long
ebb. Broadway had filled her length with people; not
yet the most characteristic New York crowd, but the
not less interesting multitude of strangers arrived by the
early boats and trains, and that easily distinguishable
class of lately New Yorkised people from other places
about whom in the metropolis still hung the provincial
traditions of early rising; and over all, from moment to
moment, the eager, audacious, well-dressed, proper life
of the mighty city was beginning to prevail,—though this
was not so notable where Basil and Isabel had paused at
a certain window. It was the office of one of the English
steamers, and he was saying, "It was by this line I sailed,
you know,"—and she was interrupting him with "When
who could have dreamed that you would ever be telling
me of it here?" So the old marvel was wondered over
anew, till it filled the world in which there was room
for nothing but the strangeness that they should have
loved each other so long and not made it known, that
they should ever have uttered it, and that, being uttered,
it should be so much more and better than ever could
have been dreamed. The broken engagement was a fable
of disaster that only made their present fortune more
prosperous. The city ceased about them, and they walked
on up the street, the first man and the first woman in the
garden of the new-made earth. As they were both very
conscious people, they recognized in themselves some
sense of this, and presently drolled it away, in the
opulence of a time when every moment brought some
beautiful dream, and the soul could be prodigal of its
bliss.

"I think if I had the naming of the animals over again,

this morning, I shouldn't call snakes *snakes;* should you, Eve?" laughed Basil in intricate acknowledgment of his happiness.

"O no, Adam; we'd look out all the most graceful euphemisms in the newspapers, and we wouldn't hurt the feelings of a spider."

II.

THEY had waited to see Leonard, in order that they might learn better how to find his house in the country; and now, when they came in upon him at nine o'clock, he welcomed them with all his friendly heart. He rose from the pile of morning's letters to which he had just sat down; he placed them the easiest chairs; he made a feint of its not being a busy hour with him, and would have had them look upon his office, which was still damp and odorous from the porter's broom, as a kind of downtown parlour; but after they had briefly accounted to his amazement for their appearance then and there, and Isabel had boasted of the original fashion in which they had that morning seen New York, they took pity on him, and bade him adieu till evening.

They crossed from Broadway to the noisome street by the ferry, and in a little while had taken their places in the train on the thither side of the water.

"Don't tell me, Basil," said Isabel, "that Leonard travels fifty miles every day by rail going to and from his work!"

"I must, dearest, if I would be truthful."

"Then, darling, there *are* worse things in this world than living up at the South End, aren't there?" And in agreement upon Boston as a place of the greatest natural advantages, as well as all acquirable merits, with after talk that need not be recorded, they arrived in the best humour at the little country station near which the Leonards dwelt.

I must inevitably follow Mrs. Isabel thither, though I do it at the cost of the reader, who suspects the excitements which a long description of the movement would delay. The ladies were very old friends, and they had not met since Isabel's return from Europe and renewal of her engagement. Upon the news of this, Mrs. Leonard had swallowed with surprising ease all that she had said in blame of Basil's conduct during the rupture, and exacted a promise from her friend that she should pay her the first visit after their marriage. And now that they had come together, their only talk was of husbands, whom they viewed in every light to which husbands could be turned, and still found an inexhaustible novelty in the theme. Mrs. Leonard beheld in her friend's joy the sweet reflection of her own honeymoon, and Isabel was pleased to look upon the prosperous marriage of the former as the image of her future. Thus, with immense profit and comfort, they reassured one another by every question and answer, and in their weak content lapsed far behind the representative women of our age, when husbands are at best a necessary evil, and the relation of wives to them is known to be one of pitiable subjection. When these two pretty fogies put their heads of false hair together, they were as silly and benighted as their great-grandmothers could have been in the same circumstances, and, as I say, shamefully encouraged each other in their absurdity. The absurdity appeared too good and blessed to be true. "Do you really suppose, Basil," Isabel would say to her oppressor, after having given him some elegant extract from the last conversation upon husbands, "that we shall get on as smoothly as the Leonards when we have been married ten years? Lucy says that things go more hitchily the first year than ever they do afterwards, and that people love each other better and better just because they've got used to it. Well, our bliss does seem a little crude and garish compared with their happiness; and yet"—she put up both her palms against his, and gave a vehement little push—"there *is* something agreeable about it, even at this stage of the proceedings."

"Isabel," said her husband with severity, "this is bridal!"

"No matter! I only want to seem an old married woman to the general public. But the application of it is that you must be careful not to contradict me, or cross me in anything, so that we can be like the Leonards very much sooner than they became so. The great object is not to have any hitchiness; and you know you *are* provoking—at times."

They both educated themselves for continued and tranquil happiness by the example and precept of their friends; and the time passed swiftly in the pleasant learning, and in the novelty of the life led by the Leonards. This indeed merits a closer study than can be given here, for it is the life led by vast numbers of prosperous New Yorkers who love both the excitement of the city and the repose of the country, and who aspire to unite the enjoyment of both in their daily existence. The suburbs of the metropolis stretch landward fifty miles in every direction; and everywhere are handsome villas like Leonard's, inhabited by men like himself, whom strict study of the time-table enables to spend all their working hours in the city and all their smoking and sleeping hours in the country.

The home and the neighbourhood of the Leonards put on their best looks for our bridal pair, and they were charmed. They all enjoyed the visit, said guests and hosts, they were all sorry to have it come to an end; yet they all resigned themselves to this conclusion. Practically, it had no other result than to detain the travellers into the very heart of the hot weather. In that weather it was easy to do anything that did not require an active effort, and resignation was so natural with the mercury at ninety, that I am not sure but there was something sinful in it.

They had given up their cherished purpose of going to Albany by the day boat, which was represented to them in every possible phase. It would be dreadfully crowded, and whenever it stopped the heat would be insupportable. Besides it would bring them to Albany at an hour when they must either spend the night there, or push on to Niagara by the night train. "You had better go by the evening boat. It will be light almost till you reach West Point, and you'll see all the best scenery. Then you can get a good night's rest, and start fresh in the morning." So they were counselled, and they assented, as they would have done if they had been advised: "You had better go by the morning boat. It's deliciously cool, travelling; you see the whole of the river; you reach Albany for supper, and you push through to Niagara that night and are done with it."

They took leave of Leonard at breakfast and of his wife at noon, and fifteen minutes later they were rushing from the heat of the country into the heat of the city, where some affairs and pleasures were to employ them till the evening boat should start.

Their spirits were low, for the terrible spell of the great heat brooded upon them. ' All abroad burned the fierce white light of the sun, in which not only the earth seemed to parch and thirst, but the very air withered, and was faint and thin to the troubled respiration. Their train was full of people who had come long journeys from broiling cities of the West, and who were dusty and ashen and reeking in the slumbers at which some of them still vainly caught. On every one lay an awful languor. Here and there stirred a fan, like the broken wing of a dying bird; now and then a sweltering young mother shifted her hot baby from one arm to another; after every station the desperate conductor swung through the long aisle and punched the ticket, which each passenger seemed to yield him with a tacit malediction; a suffering child hung about the empty tank, which could only gasp out a cindery drop or two of ice-water. The wind buffeted faintly at the windows; when the door was opened, the clatter of the rails struck through and through the car like a demoniac yell.

Yet when they arrived at the station by the ferry-side, they seemed to have entered its stifling darkness from fresh and vigorous atmosphere, so close and dead and mixed with the carbonic breath of the locomotives was the air of the place. The thin old wooden walls that shut out the glare of the sun transmitted an intensified warmth; the roof seemed to hover lower and lower, and in its coal-smoked, raftery hollow to generate a heat deadlier than that poured upon it from the skies.

In a convenient place in the station hung a ther-

mometer, before which every passenger, on going aboard
the ferry-boat, paused as at a shrine, and mutely paid
his devotions. At the altar of this fetich our friends also
paused, and saw that the mercury was above ninety, and,
exulting with the pride that savages take in the cruel
might of their idols, bowed their souls to the great god
Heat.

On the boat they found a place where the breath of
the sea struck cool across their faces, and made them forget the thermometer for the brief time of the transit.
But presently they drew near that strange, irregular row
of wooden buildings and jutting piers which skirts the
river on the New York side, and before the boat's motion
ceased the air grew thick and warm again, and tainted
with the foulness of the street on which the buildings
front. Upon this the boat's passengers issued, passing
up through a gangway, on one side of which a throng of
return-passengers was pent by a gate of iron bars, like a
herd of wild animals. They were streaming with perspiration, and, according to their different temperaments,
had faces of deep crimson or deadly pallor.

"Now the question is, my dear," said Basil when, free
of the press, they lingered for a moment in the shade outside, "whether we had better walk up to Broadway, at an
immediate sacrifice of fibre, and get a stage there, or take
one of these cars here, and be landed a little nearer, with
half the exertion. By this route we shall have sights and
smells which the other can't offer us, but whichever we
take we shall be sorry"

"Then I say take this," decided Isabel. "I want to be
sorry upon the easiest possible terms, this weather."

They hailed the first car that passed, and got into it.

Well for them both if she could have exercised this
philosophy with regard to the whole day's business, or if
she could have given up her plans for it with the same
resignation she had practised in regard to the day boat!
It seems to me a proof of the small advance our race has
made in true wisdom, that we find it so hard to give up
doing anything we have meant to do. It matters very
little whether the affair is one of enjoyment or of business, we feel the same bitter need of pursuing it to the
end. The mere fact of intention gives it a flavour of
duty; and dutiolatry, as one may call the devotion, has
passed so deeply into our life that we have scarcely a
sense any more of the sweetness of even a neglected
pleasure. We will not taste the fine, guilty rapture of
a deliberate dereliction; the gentle sin of omission is all
but blotted from the calendar of our crimes. If I had
been Columbus, I should have thought twice before setting sail, when I was quite ready to do so; and as for
Plymouth Rock, I should have sternly resisted the
blandishments of those twin sirens, Starvation and Cold,
who beckoned the Puritans shoreward, and as soon as
ever I came in sight of their granite perch should have
turned back to England. But it is now too late to repair
these errors, and so, on one of the hottest days of last
year, behold my obdurate bridal pair, in a Tenth or
Twentieth Avenue horse-car, setting forth upon the fulfilment of a series of intentions, any of which had wiselier
been left unaccomplished. Isabel had said they would
call upon certain people 'in Fiftieth Street, and then
shop slowly down, ice-creaming and staging and variously cooling and calming by the way, until they reached the
ticket-office on Broadway, whence they could indefinitely

betake themselves to the steamboat an hour or two before her departure. She felt that they had yielded sufficiently to circumstances and conditions already on this journey, and she was resolved that the present half-day in New York should be the half-day of her original design.

It was not the most advisable thing, as I have allowed, but it was inevitable, and it afforded them a spectacle which is by no means wanting in sublimity, and which is certainly unique,—the spectacle of that great city on a hot day, defiant of the elements, and prospering on with every form of labour, and at a terrible cost of life. The man carrying the hod to the top of the walls that rankly grow and grow as from his life's blood, will only lay down his load when he feels the mortal glare of the sun blaze in upon heart and brain; the plethoric millionaire for whom he toils will plot and plan in his office till he swoons at the desk; the trembling beast must stagger forward while the flame-faced tormentor on the box has strength to lash him on; in all those vast palaces of commerce there are ceaseless sale and purchase, packing and unpacking, lifting up and laying down, arriving and departing loads; in thousands of shops is the unspared and unsparing weariness of selling; in the street, filled by the hurry and suffering of tens of thousands, is the weariness of buying.

Their afternoon's experience was something that Basil and Isabel could, when it was past, look upon only as a kind of vision, magnificent at times, and at other times full of indignity and pain. They seemed to have dreamed of a long horse-car pilgrimage through that squalid street by the river-side, where presently they came to a market, opening upon the view hideous vistas of car-

nage, and then into a wide avenue, with processions of
cars like their own coming and going up and down the
centre of a foolish and useless breadth, which made even
the tall buildings (rising gauntly up among the older
houses of one or two stories) on either hand look low,
and let in the sun to bake the dust that the hot breaths
of wind caught up and sent swirling into the shabby
shops. Here they dreamed of the eternal demolition
and construction of the city, and further on of vacant
lots full of granite boulders, clambered over by goats.
In their dream they had fellow-passengers, whose sufferings made them odious, and whom they were glad to
leave behind when they alighted from the car, and running out of the blaze of the avenue, quenched themselves
in the shade of the cross-street. A little strip of shadow
lay along the row of brown-stone fronts, but there were
intervals where the vacant lots cast no shadow. With
great bestowal of thought they studied hopelessly how
to avoid these spaces as if they had been difficult torrents
or vast expanses of desert sand: they crept slowly along
till they came to such a place, and dashed swiftly across
it, and then, fainter than before, moved on. They seemed
now and then to stand at doors, and to be told that
people were out, and again that they were in; and they
had a sense of cool dark parlours, and the airy rustling
of light-muslined ladies, of chat and of fans and ice-
water, and then they came forth again; and evermore

"The day increased from heat to heat."

At last they were aware of an end of their visits, and
of a purpose to go down town again, and of seeking the
nearest car by endless blocks of brown-stone fronts,

which with their eternal brown-stone flights of steps,
and their handsome, intolerable uniformity, oppressed
them like a procession of houses trying to pass a given
point and never getting by. Upon these streets there
was seldom a soul to be seen, so that when their ringing
at a door had evoked answer, it had startled them with
a vague, sad surprise. In the distance on either hand
they could see cars and carts and wagons toiling up and
down the avenues, and on the next intersecting pavement sometimes a labourer with his jacket slung across
his shoulder, or a dog that had plainly made up his mind
to go mad. Up to the time of their getting into one of
these phantasmal cars for the return down-townwards
they had kept up a show of talk in their wretched
dream; they had spoken of other hot days that they had
known elsewhere; and they had wondered that the
tragical character of heat had been so little recognized.
They said that the daily New York murder might even
at that moment be somewhere taking place; and that
no murder of the whole homicidal year could have such
proper circumstance; they morbidly wondered what
that day's murder would be, and in what swarming
tenement-house, or den of the assassin streets by the
river-sides,—if indeed it did not befall in some such high,
close-shuttered, handsome dwelling as those they passed,
in whose twilight it would be so easy to strike down the
master and leave him undiscovered and unmourned by
the family ignorantly absent at the mountains or the sea-
side. They conjectured of the horror of midsummer
battles, and pictured the anguish of ship-wrecked men
upon a tropical coast, and the grimy misery of stevedores
unloading shiny cargoes of anthracite coal at city docks.

But now at last, as they took seats opposite one another
in the crowded car, they seemed to have drifted infinite
distances and long epochs asunder.   They looked hopelessly across the intervening gulf, and mutely ques-
tioned when it was and from what far city they or some
remote ancestors of theirs had set forth upon a wedding
journey.   They bade each other a tacit farewell, and
with patient, pathetic faces awaited the end of the
world.

When they alighted, they took their way up through
one of the streets of the great wholesale businesses, to
Broadway.   On this street was a throng of trucks and
wagons lading and unlading; bales and boxes rose and
sank by pulleys overhead; the footway was a labyrinth
of packages of every shape and size; there was no flag-
ging of the pitiless energy that moved all forward, no
sign of how heavy a weight lay on it, save in the reeking
faces of its helpless instruments.   But when the wedding-
journeyers emerged upon Broadway, the other passages
and incidents of their dream faded before the superior
fantasticality of the spectacle.   It was four o'clock, the
deadliest hour of the deadly summer day.   The spirit-
less air seemed to have a quality of blackness in it, as if
filled with the gloom of low-hovering wings.   One half
the street lay in shadow, and one half in sun; but the
sunshine itself was dim, as if a heat greater than its own
had smitten it with languor.   Little gusts of sick, warm
wind blew across the great avenue at the corners of the
intersecting streets.   In the upward distance, at which
the journeyers looked, the loftier roofs and steeples lifted
themselves dim out of the livid atmosphere, and far up
and down the length of the street swept a stream of tor-

mented life. All sorts of wheeled things thronged it, conspicuous among which rolled and jarred the gaudily painted stages, with quivering horses driven each by a man who sat in the shade of a branching white umbrella, and suffered with a moody truculence of aspect, and as if he harboured the bitterness of death in his heart for the crowding passengers within, when one of them pulled the strap about his legs, and summoned him to halt. Most of the foot-passengers kept to the shady side, and to the unaccustomed eyes of the strangers they were not less in number than at any other time, though there were fewer women among them. Indomitably resolute of soul, they held their course with the swift pace of custom, and only here and there they showed the effect of the heat. One man, collarless, with waistcoat unbuttoned, and hat set far back from his forehead, waved a fan before his death-white flabby face, and set down one foot after the other with the heaviness of a somnambulist. Another, as they passed him, was saying huskily to the friend at his side, "I can't stand this much longer. My hands tingle as if they had gone to sleep; my heart"— But still the multitude hurried on, passing, repassing, encountering, evading, vanishing into shop-doors and emerging from them, dispersing down the side streets, and swarming out of them. It was a scene that possessed the beholder with singular fascination, and in its effect of universal lunacy, it might well have seemed the last phase of a world presently to be destroyed. They who were in it but not of it, as they fancied,—though there was no reason for this,—looked on it amazed, and at last their own errands being accomplished, and themselves so far cured of the madness of purpose, they cried

D

with one voice, that it was a hideous sight, and strove to
take refuge from it in the nearest place where the soda-
fountain sparkled. It was a vain desire. At the front
door of the apothecary's hung a thermometer, and as
they entered they heard the next comer cry out with a
maniacal pride in the affliction laid upon mankind,
"Ninety-seven degrees!" Behind them at the door
there poured in a ceaseless stream of people, each pausing at the shrine of heat, before he tossed off the hissing
draught that two pale, close-clipped boys served them
from either side of the fountain. Then in the order of
their coming they issued through another door upon the
side street, each, as he disappeared, turning his face half
round, and casting a casual glance upon a little group
near another counter. The group was of a very patient,
half-frightened, half-puzzled looking gentleman who sat
perfectly still on a stool, and of a lady who stood beside
him, rubbing all over his head a handkerchief full of
pounded ice, and easing one hand with the other when
the first became tired. Basil drank his soda and paused
to look upon this group, which he felt would commend
itself to realistic sculpture as eminently characteristic of
the local life, and as "The Sunstroke" would sell
enormously in the hot season. "Better take a little more
of that," the apothecary said, looking up from his prescription, and, as the organized sympathy of the seemingly indifferent crowd, smiling very kindly at his
patient, who thereupon tasted something in the glass he
held. "Do you still feel like fainting?" asked the humane
authority. "Slightly, now and then," answered the
other, "but I'm hanging on hard to the bottom curve of
that icicled S on your soda-fountain, and I feel that I'm

all right as long as I can see that. The people get rather hazy, occasionally, and have no features to speak of. But I don't know that I look very impressive myself," he added in the jesting mood which seems the natural condition of Americans in the face of all embarrassments.

"O, you'll do" the apothecary answered, with a laugh; but he said, in answer to an anxious question from the lady, "He mustn't be moved for an hour yet," and gaily pestled away at a prescription, while she resumed her office of grinding the pounded ice round and round upon her husband's skull. Isabel offered her the commiseration of friendly words, and of looks kinder yet, and then seeing that they could do nothing, she and Basil fell into the endless procession, and passed out of the side door. "What a shocking thing!" she whispered. "Did you see how all the people looked, one after another, so indifferently at that couple, and evidently forgot them the next instant? It was dreadful. I shouldn't like to have you sun-struck in New York."

"That's very considerate of you; but place for place, if any accident must happen to me among strangers, I think I should prefer to have it in New York. The biggest place is always the kindest as well as the cruellest place. Amongst the thousands of spectators the good Samaritan as well as the Levite would be sure to be. As for a sun-stroke, it requires peculiar gifts. But if you compel me to a choice in the matter, then I say, give me the busiest part of Broadway for a sun-stroke. There is such experience of calamity there that you could hardly fall the first victim to any misfortune. Probably the gentleman at the apothecary's was merely exhausted by the heat, and ran in there for revival. The apothecary has a case of the kind on his hands every blazing afternoon, and knows just what to do. The crowd may be a little *ennuyé* of sun-strokes, and to that degree indifferent, but they most likely know that they can only do harm by an expression of sympathy, and so they delegate their pity as they have delegated their helpfulness to the proper authority, and go about their business. If a man was overcome in the middle of a village street, the blundering country druggist wouldn't know what to do, and the tender-hearted people would crowd about so that no breath of air could reach the victim."

"May be so, dear," said the wife, pensively; "but if anything did happen to you in New York, I should like to have the spectators look as if they saw a human being in trouble. Perhaps I'm a little exacting."

"I think you are. Nothing is so hard as to understand that there are human beings in this world besides one's self and one's set. But let us be selfishly thankful that it isn't you and I there in the apothecary's shop, as it might very well be; and let us get to the boat as soon as we can, and end this horrible midsummer-day's dream. We must have a carriage," he added with tardy wisdom, hailing an empty hack, "as we ought to have had all day; though I'm not sorry, now the worst's over, to have seen the worst."

III.

THE NIGHT BOAT

THERE is little proportion about either pain or pleasure; a headache darkens the universe while it lasts, a cup of tea really lightens the spirit bereft of all reasonable consolations. Therefore I do not think it trivial or untrue to say that there is for the moment nothing more satisfactory in life than to have bought your ticket on the night boat up the Hudson and secured your stateroom key an hour or two before departure, and some time even before the pressure at the clerk's office has begun. In the transaction with this castellated baron, you have of course been treated with haughtiness, but not with ferocity, and your self-respect swells with a sense of having escaped positive insult; your key clicks cheerfully in your pocket against its gutta-percha number, and you walk up and down the gorgeously carpeted, single-columned, two-story cabin, amid a multitude of plush sofas and chairs, a glitter of glass, and a tinkle of prismatic chandeliers overhead, unawed even by the aristocratic gloom of the yellow waiters. Your own state-room as you enter it from time to time is an ever-new surprise of splendours, a magnificent effect of amplitude, of mahogany bedstead, of lace curtains, and of marble-topped wash-stand. In the mere wantonness of an unalloyed prosperity you say to the saffron nobleman nearest your door, "Bring me a

pitcher of ice-water, quick, please!" and you do not find
the half-hour that he is gone very long.

If the ordinary wayfarer experiences so much pleasure
from these things, then imagine the infinite comfort of
our wedding-journeyers, transported from Broadway on
that pitiless afternoon to the shelter and the quiet of
that absurdly palatial steamboat. It was not yet crowded, and by the river-side there was almost a freshness in
the air. They disposed of their troubling bags and packages; they complimented the ridiculous princeliness of
their state-room, and then they betook themselves to
the sheltered space aft of the saloon, where they sat down
for the tranquiller observance of the wharf and whatever should come to be seen by them. Like all people
who have just escaped with their lives from some menac-
ing calamity, they were very philosophical in spirit; and
having got aboard of their own motion, and being
neither of them apparently the worse for the ordeal they
had passed through, were of a light, conversational
temper.

"What an amusingly superb affair!" Basil cried as
they glanced through an open window down the long
vista of the saloon. "Good heavens! Isabel, does it take
all this to get us plain republicans to Albany in comfort
and safety, or are we really a nation of princes in dis-
guise? Well, I shall never be satisfied with less here-
after," he added. "I am spoilt for ordinary paint and
upholstery from this hour; I am a ruinous spendthrift,
and a humble three-story swell-front up at the South
End is no longer the place for me. Dearest,

"Let us swear an oath, and keep it with an equal mind."

never to leave this Aladdin's-palace-like steamboat, but

spend our lives in perpetual trips up and down the Hudson."

To which not very costly banter Isabel responded in kind, and rapidly sketched the life they could lead aboard. Since they could not help it, they mocked the public provision which, leaving no interval between disgraceful squalor and ludicrous splendour, accommodates our democratic *ménage* to the taste of the richest and most extravagant plebeian amongst us. He, unhappily, minds danger and oppression as little as he minds money, so long as he has a spectacle and a sensation, and it is this ruthless imbecile who will have lace curtains to the steamboat berth into which he gets with his pantaloons on, and out of which he may be blown by an exploding boiler at any moment; it is he who will have for supper that overgrown and shapeless dinner in the lower saloon, and will not let any one else buy tea or toast for a less sum than he pays for his surfeit; it is he who perpetuates the insolence of the clerk and the reluctance of the waiters; it is he, in fact, who now comes out of the saloon, with his womankind, and takes chairs under the awning where Basil and Isabel sit. Personally, he is not so bad; he is good-looking, like all of us; he is better dressed than most of us; he behaves himself quietly, if not easily; and no lord so loathes a scene. Next year he is going to Europe, where he will not show to so much advantage as here; but for the present it would be hard to say in what way he is vulgar, and perhaps vulgarity is not so common a thing after all.

It was something besides the river that made the air so much more sufferable than it had been. Over the city, since our friends had come aboard the boat, a black cloud had gathered and now hung low upon it, while the wind from the face of the water took the dust in the neighbouring streets, and frolicked it about the house-tops, and in the faces of the arriving passengers, who, as the moment of departure drew near, appeared in constantly increasing numbers and in greater variety, with not only the trepidation of going upon them, but also with the electrical excitement people feel before a tempest. The breast of the black cloud was now zigzagged from moment to moment by lightning, and claps of deafening thunder broke from it. At last the long endurance of the day was spent, and out of its convulsion burst floods of rain, again and again sweeping the promenade-deck where the people sat, and driving them disconsolate into the saloon. The air was darkened as by night, and with many regrets for the vanishing prospect, mingled with a sense of relief from the heat, our friends felt the boat tremble away from her moorings and set forth upon her trip.

"Ah! if we had only taken the day boat!" moaned Isabel. "Now we shall see nothing of the river landscape, and we shall never be able to put ourselves down when we long for Europe, by declaring that the scenery of the Hudson is much finer than that of the Rhine."

Yet they resolved, this indomitably good-natured couple, that they would be just even to the elements, which had by no means been generous to them; and they owned that if so noble a storm had celebrated their departure upon some storied river from some more romantic port than New York, they would have thought it an admirable thing. Even whilst they contented themselves, the storm passed, and left a veiled and

humid sky overhead, that gave a charming softness to
the scene on which their eyes fell when they came out
of the saloon again, and took their places with a largely
increased companionship on the deck.

They had already reached that part of the river where
the uplands begin, and their course was between stately
walls of rocky steepness, or wooded slopes, or grassy
hollows, the scene for ever losing and taking grand and
lovely shape. Wreaths of mist hung about the tops of
the loftier headlands, and long shadows draped their
sides. As the night grew, lights twinkled from a lonely
house here and there in the valleys; a swarm of lamps
showed a town where it lay upon the lap or at the foot
of the hills. Behind them stretched the great grey river,
haunted with many sails; now a group of canal-boats
grappled together, and having an air of cosiness in their
adventure upon this strange current out of their own
sluggish waters, drifted out of sight; and now a smaller
and slower steamer, making a laborious show of keeping
up was passed, and reluctantly fell behind; along the
water's edge rattled and hooted the frequent trains.
They could not tell at any time what part of the river
they were on, and they could not, if they would, have
made its beauty a matter of conscientious observation;
but all the more, therefore, they deeply enjoyed it without
reference to time or place. They felt some natural pain
when they thought that they might unwittingly pass the
scenes that Irving has made part of the common dream-
land, and they would fain have seen the lighted windows
of the house out of which a cheerful ray has penetrated
to so many hearts; but being sure of nothing, as they
were, they had the comfort of finding the Tappan Zee

in every expanse of the river, and of discovering Sunny-
Side on every pleasant slope. By virtue of this helplessness, the Hudson, without ceasing to be the Hudson, became from moment to moment all fair and stately streams
upon which they had voyaged or read of voyaging, from
the Nile to the Mississippi. There is no other travel like
river travel; it is the perfection of movement, and one
might well desire never to arrive at one's destination.
The abundance of room, the free, pure air, the constant
delight of the eyes in the changing landscape, the soft
tremor of the boat, so steady upon her keel, the variety
of the little world on board,—all form a charm which no
good heart in a sound body can resist. So, whilst the
twilight held, well content, in contiguous chairs, they
purred in flattery of their kindly fate, imagining different pleasures, certainly, but none greater, and tasting
to its subtlest flavour the happiness conscious of itself.

Their own satisfaction, indeed, was so interesting to
them in this objective light, that they had little desire
to turn from its contemplation to the people around
them; and when at last they did so, it was still with
lingering glances of self-recognition and enjoyment.
They divined rightly that one of the main conditions of
their present felicity was the fact that they had seen so
much of time and of the world, that they had no longer
any desire to take beholding eyes, or to make any sort
of impressive figure, and they understood that their
prosperous love accounted as much as years and travel
for this result. If they had had a loftier opinion of
themselves, their indifference to others might have made
them offensive; but with their modest estimate of their

own value in the world, they could have all the comfort of self-sufficiency, without its vulgarity.

"O yes!" said Basil, in answer to some apostrophe to their bliss from Isabel, "it's the greatest imaginable satisfaction to have lived past certain things. I always knew that I was not a very handsome or otherwise captivating person, but I can remember years—now blessedly remote —when I never could see a young girl without hoping she would mistake me for something of that sort. I couldn't help desiring that some fascination of mine, which had escaped my own analysis, would have an effect upon her. I daresay all young men are so. I used to live for the possible interest I might inspire in your sex, Isabel. They controlled my movements, my attitudes; they forbade me repose; and yet I believe I was no ass, but a tolerably sensible fellow. Blessed be marriage, I am free at last! All the loveliness that exists outside of you, dearest,—and it's mighty little,— is mere pageant to me; and I thank Heaven that I can meet the most stylish girl now upon the broad level of our common humanity. Besides, it seems to me that our experience of life has quieted us in many other ways. What a luxury it is to sit here, and reflect that we do not want any of these people to suppose us rich, or distinguished, or beautiful, or well dressed, and do not care to show off in any sort of way before them!"

This content was heightened, no doubt, by a just sense of their contrast to the group of people nearest them,— a young man of the second or third quality and two young girls. The eldest of these was carrying on a vivacious flirtation with the young man, who was apparently an acquaintance of brief standing; the other was scarcely

more than a child, and sat somewhat abashed at the
sparkle of the colloquy. They were, conjecturally,
sisters going home from some visit, and not skilled in the
world, but of a certain repute in their country neighbourhood for beauty and wit. The young man presently
gave himself out as one who, in pursuit of trade for the
dry-goods house he represented, had travelled many
thousands of miles in all parts of the country. The
encounter was visibly that kind of adventure which both
would treasure up for future celebration to their different friends; and it had a brilliancy and interest
which they could not even now consent to keep to themselves. They talked to each other and at all the company within hearing, and exchanged curt speeches which
had for them all the sensation of repartee.

Young Man.—They say that beauty unadorned is
adorned the most.

Young Woman (bridling, and twitching her head
from side to side, in the high excitement of the dialogue).
—Flattery is out of place.

Young Man.—Well, never mind. If you don't believe
me, you ask your mother when you get home.

(Titter from the younger sister.)

Young Woman (scornfully).—Umph! my mother has
no control over me!

Young Man.—Nobody else has, either, *I* should say.
(Admiringly.)

Young Woman.—Yes, you've told the truth for once,
for a wonder. I'm able to take care of myself,—perfectly.
(Almost hoarse with a sense of sarcastic performance.)

Young Man.—"Whole team and big dog under the
wagon," as they say out West.

Young Woman.—Better a big dog than a puppy, *any* day.

(Giggles and horror from the younger sister, sensation on the young man, and so much rapture in the young woman that she drops the key of her state-room from her hand. They both stop, and a jocose scuffle for it ensues, after which the talk takes an autobiographical turn on the part of the young man, and drops into an unintelligible murmur. Ah! poor Real Life, which I love, can I make others share the delight I find in thy foolish and insipid face?)

Not far from this group sat two Hebrews, one young and the other old, talking of some business out of which the latter had retired. The younger had been asked his opinion upon some point, and he was expanding with a flattered consciousness of the elder's perception of his importance, and toadying to him with the pleasure which all young men feel in winning the favour of seniors in their vocation. "Well, as I was a-say'n', Isaac don't seem to haf no natcheral pent for the glothing business. Man gomes in and wands a goat,"—he seemed to be speaking of a garment and not a domestic animal,— "Isaac'll zell him the goat he wands him to puy, and he'll make him pelieve it's the goat he was a lookin' for. Well, now, that's well enough as far as it goes; but *you* know and *I* know, Mr. Rosenthal, that that's no way to do business. A man gan't zugzeed that goes upon that brincible. Id's wrong. Id's easy enough to make a man puy the goat you wand him to, if he wands a goat, but the thing is to *make him puy the goat that you wand to zell when he don't wand no goat at all.* You've asked

me what I thought, and I've dold you. Isaac'll never
zugzeed in the redail glothing-business in the world!"

"Well," sighed the elder, who filled his arm-chair quite
full, and quivered with a comfortable jelly-like tremor
in it, at every pulsation of the engine, "I was afraid of
something of the kind. As you say, Benjamin, he don't
seem to have no pent for it. And yet I proughd him up
to the business; I drained him to it, myself."

Besides these talkers, there were scattered singly, or
grouped about in twos and threes and fours, the various
people one encounters on a Hudson River boat, who are
on the whole different from the passengers on other
rivers, though they all have features in common. There
was that man of the sudden gains, who has already been
typified; and there was also the smoother rich man of
inherited wealth, from whom you can somehow know the
former so readily. They were each attended by their
several retinues of womankind, the daughters all much
alike, but the mothers somewhat different. They were
going to Saratoga, where perhaps the exigencies of
fashion would bring them acquainted, and where the
blue blood of a quarter of a century would be kind to the
yesterday's fluid of warmer hue. There was something
pleasanter in the face of the hereditary aristocrat, but
not so strong, nor, altogether, so admirable; particularly
if you reflected that he really represented nothing in the
world, no great culture, no political influence, no civic
aspiration, not even a pecuniary force, nothing but a
social set, an alien club-life, a tradition of dining. We
live in a true fairyland after all, where the hoarded
treasure turns to a heap of dry leaves. The almighty
dollar defeats itself, and finally buys nothing that a man

cares to have. The very highest pleasure that such an American's money can purchase is exile, and to this rich man doubtless Europe is a twice-told tale. Let us clap our empty pockets, dearest reader, and be glad.

We can be as glad, apparently, and with the same reason as the poorly dressed young man standing near beside the guard, whose face Basil and Isabel chose to fancy that of a poet, and concerning whom they romanced that he was going home, wherever his home was, with the manuscript of a rejected book in his pocket. They imagined him no great things of a poet, to be sure, but his pensive face claimed delicate feeling for him, and a graceful, sombre fancy, and they conjectured unconsciously caught flavours of Tennyson and Browning in his verse, with a moderner tint from Morris; for was it not a story out of mythology, with gods and heroes of the nineteenth century, that he was now carrying back from New York with him? Basil sketched from the colours of his own long-accepted disappointments a moving little picture of this poor imagined poet's adventures; with what kindness and unkindness he had been put to shame by publishers, and how, descending from his high hopes of a book, he had tried to sell to the magazines some of the shorter pieces out of the "And other Poems" which were to have filled up the volume. "He's going back rather stunned and bewildered; but it's something to have tasted the city, and its bitter may turn to sweet on his palate, at last, till he finds himself longing for the tumult that he abhors now. Poor fellow! one compassionate cut-throat of a publisher even asked him to lunch, being struck, as we are, with something fine in his face. I hope he's got somebody who believes in him, at home. Otherwise he'd be more comfortable, for the present, if he went over the railing there."

So the play of which they were both actors and spectators went on about them. Like all passages of life, it seemed now a grotesque mystery, with a bluntly enforced moral, now a farce of the broadest, now a latent tragedy folded in the disguises of comedy. All the elements, indeed, of either were at work there, and this was but one brief scene of the immense complex drama which was to proceed so variously in such different times and places, and has its *dénouement* only in eternity. The contrasts were sharp; each group had its travesty in some other; the talk of one seemed the rude burlesque, the bitter satire of the next; but of all these parodies none was so terribly effective as the two women, who sat in the midst of the company, yet were somehow distinct from the rest. One wore the deepest black of widowhood, the other was dressed in bridal white, and they were both alike awful in their mockery of guiltless sorrow and guiltless joy. They were not old, but the soul of youth was dead in their pretty, lamentable faces, and ruin ancient as sin looked from their eyes; their talk and laughter seemed the echo of an innumerable multitude of the lost haunting the world in every land and time, each solitary for ever, yet all bound together in the unity of an imperishable slavery and shame.

What a stale effect! What hackneyed characters! Let us be glad the night drops her curtain upon the cheap spectacle, and shuts these with the other actors from our view.

Within the cabin, through which Basil and Isabel now

slowly moved, there were numbers of people lounging about on the sofas, in various attitudes of talk or vacancy; and at the tables there were others reading "Lothair," a new book in the remote epoch of which I write, and a very fashionable book indeed. There was in the air that odour of paint and carpet which prevails on steamboats; the glass drops of the chandeliers ticked softly against each other, as the vessel shook with her respiration, like a comfortable sleeper, and imparted a delicious feeling of cosiness and security to our travellers.

A few hours later they struggled awake at the sharp sound of the pilot's bell signalling the engineer to slow the boat. There was a moment of perfect silence; then all the drops of the chandeliers in the saloon clashed musically together; then fell another silence; and at last came wild cries for help, strongly qualified with blasphemies and curses. "Send out a boat!" "There was a woman aboard that steamboat!" "Lower your boats!" "Run a craft right down, with your big boat!" "Send out a boat and pick up the crew!" The cries rose and sank, and finally ceased; through the lattice of the stateroom window some lights shone faintly on the water at a distance.

"Wait here, Isabel" said her husband. "We've run down a boat. We don't seem hurt; but I'll go see. I'll be back in a minute."

Isabel had emerged into a world of dishabille, a world wildly unbuttoned and unlaced, where it was the fashion for ladies to wear their hair down their backs, and to walk about in their stockings, and to speak to each other without introduction. The place with which she had felt so familiar a little while before was now utterly
E

estranged. There was no motion of the boat, and in the
momentary suspense a quiet prevailed, in which those
grotesque shapes of disarray crept noiselessly round
whispering panic-stricken conjectures. There was no
rushing to and fro, nor tumult of any kind, and there
was not a man to be seen, for apparently they had all
gone like Basil to learn the extent of the calamity. A
mist of sleep involved the whole, and it was such a topsy-
turvy world that it would have seemed only another
dream-land, but that it was marked for reality by one
signal fact. With the rest appeared the woman in bridal
white and the woman in widow's black, and there, amidst
the fright that made all others friends, and for aught
that most knew, in the presence of death itself, these two
moved together shunned and friendless.

Somehow, even before Basil returned, it had become
known to Isabel and the rest that their own steamer had
suffered no harm, but that she had struck and sunk
another convoying a flotilla of canal-boats, from which
those alarming cries and curses had come. The steamer
was now lying by for the small boats she had sent out to
pick up the crew of the sunken vessel.

"Why, I only heard a little tinkling of the chandeliers," said one of the ladies. "Is it such a very slight
matter to run down another boat and sink it?"

She appealed indirectly to Basil, who answered lightly,
"I don't think you ladies ought to have been disturbed at
all. In running over a common tow-boat on a perfectly
clear night like this there should have been no noise
and no perceptible jar. They manage better on the
Mississippi, and both boats often go down without waking the lightest sleeper on board."

The ladies, perhaps from a deficient sense of humor, listened with undisguised displeasure to this speech. It dispersed them, in fact; some turned away to bivouac for the rest of the night upon the arm-chairs and sofas, while others returned to their rooms. With the latter went Isabel. "Lock me in, Basil," she said, with a bold meekness, "and if anything more happens don't wake me till the last moment." It was hard to part from him, but she felt that his vigil would somehow be useful to the boat, and she confidingly fell into a sleep that lasted till daylight.

Meantime, her husband, on whom she had tacitly devolved so great a responsibility, went forward to the promenade in front of the saloon, in hopes of learning something more of the catastrophe from the people whom he had already found gathered there.

A large part of the passengers were still there, seated or standing about in earnest colloquy. They were in that mood which follows great excitement, and in which the feeblest-minded are sure to lead the talk. At such times one feels that a sensible frame of mind is unsympathetic, and if expressed, unpopular, or perhaps not quite safe; and Basil, warned by his fate with the ladies, listened gravely to the voice of the common imbecility and incoherence.

The principal speaker was a tall person wearing a silk travelling-cap. He had a face of stupid benignity and a self-satisfied smirk; and he was formally trying to put at his ease, and hopelessly confusing, the loutish youth before him. "You say you saw the whole accident, and you're probably the only passenger that did see it. You'll be the most important witness at the trial," he added, as if there would ever be any trial about it. "Now, how did the tow-boat hit us?"

"Well, she came bows on."

"Ah! bows on," repeated the other, with great satisfaction; and a little murmur of "Bows on!" ran round the listening circle.

"That is," added the witness, "it seemed as if we struck her amidships, and cut her in two, and sunk her."

"Just so," continued the examiner, accepting the explanation, "bows on. Now I want to ask if you saw our captain or any of the crew about?"

"Not a soul," said the witness, with the solemnity of a man already on oath.

"That'll do," exclaimed the other. "This gentleman's experience coincides exactly with my own. I didn't see the collision, but I did see the cloud of steam from the sinking boat, and I saw her go down. There wasn't an officer to be found anywhere on board our boat. I looked about for the captain and the mate myself, and couldn't find either of them high or low."

"The officers ought all to have been sitting here on the promenade deck," suggested one ironical spirit in the crowd, but no one noticed him.

The gentleman in the silk travelling-cap now took a chair, and a number of sympathetic listeners drew their chairs about him, and then began an interchange of experience, in which each related to the last particular all that he felt, thought, and said, and, if married, what his wife felt, thought, and said, at the moment of the calamity. They turned the disaster over and over in their talk, and rolled it under their tongues. Then they reverted to former accidents in which they had been concerned; and the silk-capped gentleman told, to the common admiration, of a fearful escape of his, on the Erie Road, from being thrown down a steep embankment fifty feet high by a piece of rock that had fallen on the track. "Now just see, gentlemen, what a little thing, humanly speaking, life depends upon. If that old woman had been able to sleep, and hadn't sent that boy down to warn the train, we should have run into the rock and been dashed to pieces. The passengers made up a purse for the boy, and I wrote a full account of it to the papers."

"Well," said one of the group, a man in a hard hat, "I never lie down on a steamboat or a railroad train. I want to be ready for whatever happens."

The others looked at this speaker with interest, as one who had invented a safe method of travel.

"I happened to be up to-night, but I almost always undress and go to bed, just as if I were in my own house," said the gentleman of the silk cap. "I don't say your way isn't the best, but that's my way."

The champions of the rival systems debated their merits with suavity and mutual respect, but they met with scornful silence a compromising spirit who held that it was better to throw off your coat and boots, but keep your pantaloons on. Meanwhile, the steamer was hanging idle upon the current, against which it now and then stirred a careless wheel, still waiting for the return of the small boats. Thin grey clouds, through rifts of which a star sparkled keenly here and there, veiled the heavens; shadowy bluffs loomed up on either hand; in a hollow on the left twinkled a drowsy little town; a beautiful stillness lay on all.

After an hour's interval a shout was heard from far down the river; then later the plash of oars; then a cry hailing the approaching boats, and the answer, "All safe!" Presently the boats had come alongside, and the passengers crowded down to the guard to learn the details of the search. Basil heard a hollow, moaning, gurgling sound, regular as that of the machinery, for some note of which he mistook it. "Clear the gangway there!" shouted a gruff voice; "man scalded here!" And a burden was carried by from which fluttered, with its terrible regularity, that utterance of mortal anguish.

Basil went again to the forward promenade, and sat down to see the morning come.

The boat swiftly ascended the current, and presently the steeper shores were left behind and the banks fell away in long upward sloping fields, with farm-houses and with stacks of harvest dimly visible in the generous expanses. By-and-by they passed a fisherman drawing his nets, and bending from his boat, there near Albany, N.Y., in the picturesque immortal attitudes of Raphael's Galilean fisherman; and now a flush mounted the pale face of the east, and through the dewy coolness of the dawn there came, more to the sight than any other sense, a vague menace of heat. But as yet the air was deliciously fresh and sweet, and Basil bathed his weariness in it, thinking with a certain luxurious compassion of the scalded man, and how he was to fare that day. This poor wretch seemed of another order of beings, as the calamitous always seem to the happy, and Basil's pity was quite an abstraction; which, again, amused and shocked him, and he asked his heart of bliss to consider of sorrow a little more earnestly as the lot of all men,

and not merely of an alien creature here and there.   He
dutifully tried to imagine another issue to the disaster
of the night, and to realize himself suddenly bereft of her
who so filled his life.   He bade his soul remember that,
in the security of sleep, Death had passed them both so
close that his presence might well have chilled their
dreams, as the iceberg that grazes the ship in the night
freezes all the air about it.   But it was quite idle: where
love was, life only was; and sense and spirit alike put
aside the burden that he would have laid upon them;
his reverie reflected with delicious caprice the looks, the
tones, the movements that he loved, and bore him far
away from the sad images that he had invited to mirror
themselves in it.

IV.

A DAY'S RAILROADING

HAPPINESS has commonly a good appetite; and the thought of the fortunately ended adventures of the night, the fresh morning air, and the content of their own hearts, gifted our friends, by the time the boat reached Albany, with a wholesome hunger, so that they debated with spirit the question of breakfast and the best place of breakfasting in a city which neither of them knew, save in the most fugitive and sketchy way.

They decided at last, in view of the early departure of the train, and the probability that they would be more hurried at a hotel, to breakfast at the station, and thither they went and took places at one of the many tables within, where they seemed to have been expected only by the flies. The waitress plainly had not looked for them, and for a time found their presence so incredible that she would not acknowledge the rattling that Basil was obliged to make on his glass. Then it appeared that the cook would not believe in them, and he did not send them, till they were quite faint, the peppery and muddy draught which impudently affected to be coffee, the oily slices of fugacious potatoes slipping about in their shallow dish and skilfully evading pursuit, the pieces of beef that simulated steak, the hot, greasy biscuit, steaming evilly up into the face when opened, and then soddening into masses of condensed dyspepsia.

The wedding-journeyers looked at each other with eyes of sad amaze. They bowed themselves for a moment to the viands, and then by an equal impulse refrained. They were sufficiently young, they were happy, they were hungry; nature is great and strong, but art is greater, and before these triumphs of the cook at the Albany depot appetite succumbed. By a terrible *tour de force* they swallowed the fierce and turbid liquor in their cups, and then speculated fantastically upon the character and history of the materials of that breakfast.

Presently Isabel paused, played a little with her knife, and, after a moment, looked up at her husband with an arch regard, and said: "I was just thinking of a small station somewhere in the South of France where our train once stopped for breakfast. I remember the freshness and brightness of everything on the little tables,—the plates, the napkins, the gleaming half-bottles of wine. They seemed to have been preparing that breakfast for us from the beginning of time, and we were hardly seated before they served us with great cups of *café-au-lait*, and the sweetest rolls and butter; then a delicate cutlet, with an unspeakable gravy, and potatoes,—such potatoes! Dear me, how little I ate of it! I wish, for once, I'd had your appetite, Basil; I do indeed."

She ended with a heartless laugh, in which, despite the tragical contrast her words had suggested, Basil finally joined. So much amazement had probably never been got before out of the misery inflicted in that place; but their lightness did not at all commend them. The waitress had not liked it from the first, and had served them with reluctance; and the proprietor did not like it, and kept his eye upon them as if he believed them about to escape without payment. Here, then, they had enforced a great fact of travelling,—that people who serve the public are kindly and pleasant in proportion as they serve it well. The unjust and the inefficient have always that consciousness of evil which will not let a man forgive his victim, or like him to be cheerful.

Our friends, however, did not heat themselves over the fact. There was already such heat from without, even at eight o'clock in the morning, that they chose to be as cool as possible in mind, and they placidly took their places in the train, which had been made up for departure. They had deliberately rejected the notion of a drawing-room car as affording a less varied prospect of humanity, and as being less in the spirit of ordinary American travel. Now, in reward, they found themselves quite comfortable in the common passenger-car, and disposed to view the scenery, into which they struck an hour after leaving the city, with much complacency. There was sufficient draught through the open window to make the heat tolerable, and the great brooding warmth gave to the landscape the charm which it alone can impart. It is a landscape that I greatly love for its mild beauty and tranquil picturesqueness, and it is in honour of our friends that I say they enjoyed it. There are nowhere any considerable hills, but everywhere generous slopes and pleasant hollows and the wide meadows of a grazing country, with the pretty brown Mohawk River rippling down through all, and at frequent intervals the life of the canal, now near, now far away, with the lazy boats that seem not to stir, and the horses that the train passes with a whirl, and leaves slowly stepping

forward and swiftly slipping backward. There are farms
that had once, or still have, the romance to them of
being Dutch farms,—if there is any romance in that,—
and one conjectures a Dutch thrift in their waving grass
and grain. Spaces of woodland here and there dapple
the slopes, and the cosy red farm-houses repose by the
side of their capacious red barns. Truly, there is no
ground on which to defend the idleness, and yet as the
train strives furiously onward amid these scenes of
fertility and abundance, I like in fancy, to loiter behind
it, and to saunter at will up and down the landscape. I
stop at the farm-yard gates, and sit upon the porches or
thresholds, and am served with cups of buttermilk by old
Dutch ladies who have done their morning's work and
have leisure to be knitting or sewing; or if there are no
old ladies, with decent caps upon their grey hair, then I
do not complain if the drink is brought me by some red-
cheeked, comely young girl, out of Washington Irving's
pages, with no cap on her golden braids, who mirrors my
diffidence, and takes an attitude of pretty awkwardness
while she waits till I have done drinking. In the same
easily contented spirit as I lounge through the barn-yard,
if I find the old hens gone about their family affairs, I
do not mind a meadow-lark's singing in the top of the
elm-tree beside the pump. In these excursions the watch-
dogs know me for a harmless person, and will not open
their eyes as they lie coiled up in the sun before the gate.
At all the places, I have the people keep bees, and, in the
garden full of worthy pot-herbs, such idlers in the vegetable world as hollyhocks and larkspurs and four-o'-
clocks, near a great bed in which the asparagus has gone
to sleep for the season with a dream of delicate spray

hanging over it. I walk unmolested through the farmer's
tall grass, and ride with him upon the perilous seat of
his voluble mowing-machine, and learn to my heart's
content that his name begins with Van, and that his
family has owned that farm ever since the days of the
Patroon; which I dare say is not true. Then I fall asleep
in a corner of the hay-field, and wake up on the tow-path
of the canal beside that wonderfully lean horse, whose
bones you cannot count only because they are so many.
He never wakes up, but with a faltering under-lip and
half-shut eyes, hobbles stiffly on, unconscious of his
anatomical interest.   The captain hospitably asks me
on board, with a twist of the rudder swinging the stern
of the boat up to the path, so that I can step on.   She
is laden with flour from the valley of the Genesee, and
may have started on her voyage shortly after the canal
was made.   She is succinctly manned by the captain, the
driver, and the cook, a fiery-haired lady of imperfect
temper; and the cabin, which I explore, is plainly
furnished with a cookstove and a flask of whiskey. Nothing but profane language is allowed on board; and so,
in a life of wicked jollity and ease, we glide imper-
ceptibly down the canal, unvexed by the far-off future
of arrival.

Such, I say, are my own unambitious mental pastimes,
but I am aware that less superficial spirits could not be
satisfied with them, and I do not pretend that my wedding-journeyers were so.   They cast an absurd poetry
over the landscape, they invited themselves to be reminded of passages of European travel by it; and they
placed villas and castles and palaces upon all the eligible
building-sites. Ashamed of these devices, presently, Basil

patriotically tried to reconstruct the Dutch and Indian
past of the Mohawk Valley, but here he was foiled by the
immense ignorance of his wife, who as a true American
woman, knew nothing of the history of her own country,
and less than nothing of the barbarous regions beyond
the borders of her native province. She proved a bewildering labyrinth of error concerning the events
which Basil mentioned; and she had never even heard of
the massacres by the French and Indians at Schenectady,
which he in his boyhood had known so vividly that he
was scalped every night in his dreams, and woke up in
the morning expecting to see marks of the tomahawk on
the head-board. So, failing at last to extract any sentiment from the scenes without, they turned their faces
from the window, and looked about them for amusement
within the car.

It was in all respects an ordinary carful of human
beings, and it was perhaps the more worthy to be studied
on that account. As in literature the true artist will
shun the use even of real events if they are of an improbable character, so the sincere observer of man will
not desire to look upon his heroic or occasional phrases,
but will seek him in his habitual moods of vacancy and
tiresomeness. To me, at any rate, he is at such times
very precious; and I never perceive him to be so much a
man and a brother as when I feel the pressure of his
vast, natural, unaffected dullness. Then I am able to
enter confidently into his life and inhabit there, to think
his shallow and feeble thoughts, to be moved by his
dumb, stupid desires, to be dimly illumined by his
stinted inspirations, to share his foolish prejudices, to
practice his obtuse selfishness. Yes, it is a very amusing

world, if you do not refuse to be amused; and our
friends were very willing to be entertained. They delighted in the precise, thick-fingered old ladies who
bought sweet apples of the boys come aboard with
baskets, and who were so long in finding the right change,
that our travellers, leaping in thought with the boys
from the moving train, felt that they did so at the peril
of their lives. Then they were interested in people who
went out and found their friends waiting for them, or
else did not find them, and wandered disconsolately up
and down before the country stations, carpet-bag in
hand; in women who came aboard, and were awkwardly
shaken hands with or sheepishly kissed by those who
hastily got seats for them, and placed their bags or their
babies in their laps, and turned for a nod at the door:
in young ladies who were seen to places by young men
(the latter seemed not to care if the train did go off with
them), and then threw up their windows and talked with
girl-friends on the platform without, till the train began
to move, and at last turned with gleaming eyes and moist
red lips, and panted hard in the excitement of thinking
about it, and could not calm themselves to the dull level
of the travel around them; in the conductor, coldly and
inaccessibly vigilant, as he went his rounds, reaching
blindly for the tickets with one hand while he bent his
head from time to time, and listened with a faint sarcastic smile to the questions of passengers who supposed
they were going to get some information out of him; in
the train-boy, who passed through on his many errands
with prize candies, gum-drops, pop-corn, papers and
magazines, and distributed books and the police journals
with a blind impartiality, or a prodigious ignorance, or a

supernatural perception of character in those who received them.

A through train from East to West presents some
peculiar features as well as the traits common to all railway travel; and our friends decided that this was not
a very well-dressed company, and would contrast with
the people on an express-train between Boston and New
York to no better advantage than these would show beside the average passengers between London and Paris.
And it seems true that on a westering line, the blacking
fades gradually from the boots, the hat softens and sinks,
the coat loses its rigour of cut, and the whole person
lounges into increasing informality of costume. I speak
of the undressful sex alone: woman, wherever she is
appears in the last attainable effects of fashion, which
are now all but telegraphic and universal. But most of
the passengers here were men, and they were plainly of
the free-and-easy West rather than the dapper East.
They wore faces thoughtful with the problem of buying
cheap and selling dear, and they could be known by their
silence from the loquacious, acquaintance-making way-
travellers. In these the mere coming aboard seemed to
beget an aggressively confidential mood. Perhaps they
clutched recklessly at any means of relieving their
ennui; or they felt that they might here indulge safely
in the pleasures of autobiography, so dear to all of us;
or else, in view of the many possible catastrophes, they
desired to leave some little memory of themselves behind.
At any rate, whenever the train stopped, the wedding-
journeyers caught fragments of the personal histories of
their fellow-passengers which had been rehearsing to
those that sat next the narrators. It was no more than

fair that these should somewhat magnify themselves,
and put the best complexion on their actions and the
worst upon their sufferings; that they should all appear
the luckiest or the unluckiest, the healthiest or the sick-
est, people that ever were, and should all have made or
lost the most money.   There was a prevailing desire
among them to make out that they came from or were
going to some very large place; and our friends fancied
an actual mortification in the face of a modest gentleman who got out at Penelope (or some other insignifi-
cant classical station, in the ancient Greek and Roman
part of New York State), after having listened to. the
life of a somewhat rustic-looking person who had described himself as belonging *near* New York City.

Basil also found diversion in the tender couples, who
publicly comported themelves as if in a sylvan solitude,
and, as it had been on the bank of some umbrageous
stream, far from the ken of envious or unsympathetic
eyes, reclined upon each other's shoulders and slept;
but Isabel declared that this behaviour was perfectly in-
decent.   She granted, of course, that they were foolish,
innocent people, who meant no offence, and did not feel
guilty of an impropriety, but she said that this sort of
thing was a national reproach.   If it were merely rustic
lovers, she should not care so much; but you saw people
who ought to know better, well-dressed, stylish people,
flaunting their devotion in the face of the world, and
going to sleep on each other's shoulders on every railroad train.   It was outrageous, it was scandalous, it was
really infamous.   Before she would allow herself to do
such a thing she would—well, she hardly knew what she
would not do; she would have a divorce, at any rate. She

wondered that Basil could laugh at it; and he would make her hate him if he kept on.

From the seat behind their own they were now made listeners to the history of a ten weeks' typhoid fever from the moment when the narrator noticed that he had not felt very well for a day or two back, and all at once a kind of shiver took him, till he lay fourteen days perfectly insensible, and could eat nothing but a little pounded ice—and his wife—a small woman, too—used to lift him back and forth between the bed and sofa like a feather, and the neighbours did not know half the time whether he was dead or alive. This history, from which not the smallest particular or the least significant symptom of the case was omitted, occupied an hour in recital, and was told, as it seemed, for the entertainment of one who had been five minutes before it began a stranger to the historian.

At last the train came to a stand, and Isabel wailed forth in accents of desperation the words, "O, disgusting!" The monotony of the narrative in the seat behind, fatally combining with the heat of the day, had lulled her into slumbers from which she awoke at the stopping of the train, to find her head resting tenderly upon her husband's shoulder.

She confronted his merriment with eyes of mournful rebuke; but as she could not find him, by the harshest construction, in the least to blame, she was silent.

"Never mind, dear, never mind," he coaxed, "you were really not responsible. It was fatigue, destiny, the spite of fortune,—whatever you like. In the case of the others, whom you despise so justly, I dare say it is sheer, disgraceful affection. But see that ravishing placard,

F

swinging from the roof: 'This train stops twenty minutes for dinner at Utica.' In a few minutes more we shall be at Utica. If they have anything edible there, it shall never contract *my* powers. I could dine at the Albany station, even."

In a little while they found themselves in an airy, comfortable dining-room, eating a dinner, which it seemed to them France in the flush of her prosperity need not have blushed to serve; for if it wanted a little in the last graces of art, it redeemed itself in abundance, variety, and wholesomeness. At the elbow of every famishing passenger stood a beneficent coal-black glossy fairy, in a white linen apron and jacket, serving him with that alacrity and kindliness and grace which make the negro waiter the master, not the slave of his calling, which disenthral it of servility, and constitute him your eager host, not your menial, for the moment. From table to table passed a calming influence in the person of the proprietor, who, as he took his richly earned money, checked the rising fears of the guests by repeated proclamations that there was plenty of time, and that he would give them due warning before the train started. Those who had flocked out of the cars, to prey with beak and claw, as the vulture-like fashion is, upon everything in reach, remained to eat like Christians; and even a poor, scantily-Englished Frenchman, who wasted half his time in trying to ask how long the cars stopped, and in looking at his watch, made a good dinner in spite of himself.

"O Basil, Basil!" cried Isabel, when the train was again in motion, "have we really dined once more? It seems too good to be true. Cleanliness, plenty, whole-sameness, civility! Yes, as you say, they cannot be civil where they are not just; honesty and courtesy go together; and wherever they give you outrageous things to eat, they add indigestible insults. Basil, dear, don't be jealous; I shall never meet him again; but I'm in love with that black waiter at our table. I never saw such perfect manners, such a winning and affectionate politeness. He made me feel that every mouthful I ate was a personal favour to him. What a complete gentleman! There ought never to be a white waiter. None but negroes are able to render their service a pleasure and distinction to you."

So they prattled on, doing, in their eagerness to be satisfied, a homage perhaps beyond its desert to the good dinner and the decent service of it. But here they erred in the right direction, and I find nothing more admirable in their behaviour throughout a wedding journey which certainly had its trials, than their willingness to make the very best of whatever would suffer itself to be made anything at all of. They celebrated its pleasures with magnanimous excess, they passed over its griefs with a wise forbearance. That which they found the most difficult of management was the want of incident for the most part of the time; and I who write their history might also sink under it, but that I am supported by the fact that it is so typical in this respect. I even imagine that ideal reader for whom one writes as yawning over these barren details with the life-like weariness of an actual travelling companion of theirs. Their own silence often sufficed my wedded lovers, or then, when there was absolutely nothing to engage them, they fell back upon the story of their love, which they were never tired of

hearing as they severally knew it. Let it not be a reproach to human nature or to me if I say that there was
something in the comfort of having well dined which now
touched the springs of sentiment with magical effect,
and that they had never so rejoiced in these tender
reminiscences.

They had planned to stop over at Rochester till the
morrow, that they might arrive at Niagara by daylight,
and at Utica they had suddenly resolved to make the rest
of the day's journey in a drawing-room car. The change
gave them an added reason for content; and they
realized how much they had previously sacrificed to the
idea of travelling in the most American manner, without achieving it after all, for this seemed a touch of
Americanism beyond the old-fashioned car. They reclined in luxury upon the easy-cushioned, revolving
chairs; they surveyed with infinite satisfaction the
elegance of the flying-parlour in which they sat, or turned
their contented regard through the broad plate-glass
windows upon the landscape without. They said that
none but Americans or enchanted princes in the
"Arabian Nights" ever travelled in such state; and when
the stewards of the car came round successively with
tropical fruits, ice-creams, and claret-punches, they felt
a heightened assurance that they were either enchanted
princes—or Americans. There were more ladies and
more fashion than in the other cars; and prettily dressed
children played about on the carpet; but the general
appearance of the passengers hardly suggested greater
wealth than elsewhere; and they were plainly in that
car because they were of the American race, which finds
nothing too good for it that its money can buy.

V.

THE ENCHANTED CITY, AND BEYOND

THEY knew none of the hotels in Rochester, and they had chosen a certain one in reliance upon their hand-book. When they named it there stepped forth a porter of an incredibly cordial and pleasant countenance, who took their travelling-bags, and led them to the omnibus. As they were his only passengers, the porter got inside with them, and seeing their interest in the streets through which they rode, he descanted in a strain of cheerful pride upon the city's prosperity and character, and gave the names of the people who lived in the finer houses, just as if it had been an Old-World town, and he some eager historian expecting reward for his comment upon it. He cast quite a glamour over Rochester, so that in passing a body of water, bordered by houses and overlooked by odd balconies and galleries, and crossed in the distance by a bridge upon which other houses were built, they boldly declared, being at their wit's end for a comparison, and taken with the unhoped-for picturesqueness, that it put them in mind of Verona. Thus they reached their hotel in almost a spirit of foreign travel, and very willing to verify the pleasant porter's assurance that they would like it, for everybody liked it; and it was with a sudden sinking of the heart that Basil beheld presiding over the register the conventional American hotel clerk. He

was young, he had a neat moustache and well-brushed
hair; jewelled studs sparkled in his shirt-front, and rings
on his white hands; a gentle disdain of the travelling
public breathed from his person in the mystical odours
of Ihlang ihlang. He did not lift his haughty head to
look at the wayfarer who meekly wrote his name in the
register; he did not answer him when he begged for a
cool room; he turned to the board on which the keys
hung, and, plucking one from it, slid it towards Basil on
the marble counter, touched a bell for a call-boy, whistled
a bar of Offenbach, and as he wrote the number of the
room against Basil's name, said to a friend lounging near
him, as if resuming a conversation, "Well, she's a mighty
pooty gul, any way, Chawley!"

When I reflect that this was a type of the hotel clerk
throughout the United States, that behind unnumbered
registers at this moment he is snubbing travellers into
the dust, and that they are suffering and perpetuating
him, I am lost in wonder at the national meekness. Not
that I am one to refuse the humble pie his jewelled
fingers offer me. Abjectly I take my key, and creep off
up-stairs after the call-boy, and try to give myself the
genteel air of one who has not been stepped upon. But
I think homicidal things all the same, and I rejoice that
in the safety of print I can cry out against the despot,
whom I have not the presence to defy. "You vulgar and
cruel little soul," I say, and I imagine myself breathing
the words to his teeth, "why do you treat a weary
stranger with this ignominy? I am to pay well for
what I get, and I shall not complain of that. But look
at me, and own my humanity; confess by some civil
action, by some decent phrase, that I have rights, and

that they shall be respected. Answer my proper questions; respond to my fair demands. Do not slide my key at me; do not deny me the poor politeness of a nod as you give it in my hand. I am not your equal; few men are; but I shall not presume upon your clemency. Come, I also am human."

Basil found that, for his sin in asking for a cool room, the clerk had given them a chamber into which the sun had been shining the whole afternoon; but when his luggage had been put in it seemed useless to protest, and like a true American, like you, like me, he shrank from asserting himself. When the sun went down it would be cool enough; and they turned their thoughts to supper, not venturing to hope that, as it proved, the handsome clerk was the sole blemish of the house.

Isabel viewed with innocent surprise the evidence of luxury afforded by all the appointments of a hotel so far west of Boston, and they both began to feel that natural ease and superiority which an inn always inspires in its guests, and which our great hotels, far from impairing, enhance in flattering degree; in fact, the clerk once forgotten, I protest, for my own part, I am never more conscious of my merits and riches in any other place. One has there the romance of being a stranger and a mystery to every one else, and lives in the alluring possibility of not being found out a most ordinary person.

They were so late in coming to the supper-room, that they found themselves alone in it. At the door they had a bow from the headwaiter, who ran before them and drew out chairs for them at a table, and signalled waiters to serve them, first laying before them with a gracious flourish the bill of fare.

A force of servants flocked about them, as if to contest the honour of ordering their supper; one set upon the table a heaping vase of strawberries, another flanked it with flagons of cream, a third accompanied it with cakes of varied flavour and device; a fourth obsequiously smoothed the table-cloth; a fifth, the youngest of the five, with folded arms stood by and admired the satisfaction the rest were giving. When these had been despatched for steak, for broiled white-fish of the lakes, —noblest and delicatest of the fish that swim,—for broiled chicken, for fried potatoes, for muffins, for whatever the lawless fancy, and ravening appetites of the wayfarers could suggest, this fifth waiter remained to tempt them to further excess, and vainly proposed some kind of eggs,—fried eggs, poached eggs, scrambled eggs, boiled eggs, or omelette.

"O you're sure, dearest, that this isn't a vision of fairy-land, which will vanish presently, and leave us empty and forlorn?" plaintively murmured Isabel, as the menial train reappeared, bearing the supper they had ordered, and set it smoking down.

Suddenly a look of apprehension dawned upon her face, and she let fall her knife and fork. "You *don't* think, Basil," she faltered, "that they *could* have found out we're a bridal party, and that they're serving us so magnificently because—because—O, I shall be miserable every moment we're here!" she concluded desperately.

She looked, indeed, extremely wretched for a woman with so much broiled whitefish on her plate, and such a banquet array about her; and her husband made haste to reassure her. "You're still demoralized, Isabel, by our sufferings at the Albany depot, and you exaggerate the

blessings we enjoy, though I should be sorry to under-
value them. I suspect it's the custom to use people well
at this hotel; or if we are singled out for uncom-
mon favour I think I can explain the cause. It has
been discovered by the register that we are from
Boston, and we are merely meeting the reverence,
affection, and homage which the name everywhere
commands. It's our fortune to represent for the time
being the intellectual and moral virtue of Boston. This
supper is not a tribute to you as a bride, but as a
Bostonian."

It was a cheap kind of raillery, to be sure, but it
served. It kindled the local pride of Isabel to self-de-
fence, and in the distraction of the effort she forgot her
fears; she returned with renewed appetite to the supper, and in its excellence they both let fall their dispute,
—which ended, of course, in Basil's abject confession
that Boston was the best place in the world, and nothing
but banishment could make him live elsewhere,—and
gave themselves up, as usual, to the delight of being just
what and where they were. At last, the natural course
brought them to the strawberries, and when the fifth
waiter approached from the corner of the table at which
he stood, to place the vase near them, he did not retire
at once, but presently asked if they were from the West.

Isabel smiled, and Basil answered that they were from
the East.

He faltered at this, as if doubtful of the result if he
went further, but took heart, then, and asked, "Don't
you think this is a pretty nice hotel"—hastily adding as
a concession of the probable existence of much finer
things at the East—"for a *small* hotel?"

They imagined this waiter as new to his station in life, as perhaps just arisen to it from some country tavern, and unable to repress his exultation in what seemed their sympathetic presence. They were charmed to have invited his guileless confidence, to have evoked possibly all the simple poetry of his soul; it was what might have happened in Italy, only there so much *naïveté* would have meant money; they looked at each other with rapture, and Basil answered warmly while the waiter flushed as at a personal compliment: "Yes, it's a nice hotel; one of the best I ever saw, East or West, in Europe or America."

They rose and left the room, and were bowed out by the head-waiter.

"How perfectly idyllic!" cried Isabel. "Is this Rochester, New York, or is it some vale of Arcady? Let's go out and see."

They walked out into the moonlit city, up and down streets that seemed very stately and fine, amidst a glitter of shop-window lights; and then, less of their own motion than of mere error, they quitted the business quarter, and found themselves in a quiet avenue of handsome residences,—the Beacon Street of Rochester, whatever it was called. They said it was a night and a place for lovers, for none but lovers, for lovers newly plighted, and they made believe to bemoan themselves that, hold each other dear as they would, the exultation, the thrill, the glory of their younger love was gone. Some of the houses had gardened spaces about them, from which stole, like breaths of sweetest and saddest regret, the perfume of midsummer flowers,— the despair of the rose for the bud. As they passed a certain house, a song fluttered

out of the open window and ceased, the piano warbled at
the final rush of fingers over its chords, and they saw *her*
with her fingers resting lightly on the keys, and her graceful head lifted to look into his; they saw *him* with his
arm yet stretched across to the leaves of music he had
been turning, and his face lowered to meet her gaze.

"Ah, Basil, I wish it was we, there!"

"And if they knew that we, on our wedding journey,
stood outside, would not they wish it was they, here?"

"I suppose so, dearest, and yet, once-upon-a-time was
sweet. Pass on; and let us see what charm we shall find
next in this enchanted city."

"Yes, it is an enchanted city to us," mused Basil,
aloud, as they wandered on, "and all strange cities are
enchanted. What is Rochester to the Rochesterese? A
place of a hundred thousand people, as we read in our
guide, an immense flour interest, a great railroad
entrepôt, an unrivalled nursery trade, a university, two
commercial colleges, three collegiate institutes, eight or
ten newspapers, and a free library. I dare say any respectable resident would laugh at us sentimentalizing
over his city. But Rochester is for us, who don't know it
at all, a city of any time or country, moonlit, filled with
lovers hovering over piano-fortes, of a palatial hotel with
pastoral waiters and porters,—a city of handsome streets
wrapt in beautiful quiet and dreaming of the golden age.
The only definite association with it in our minds is
the tragically romantic thought that here Sam Patch met
his fate."

"And who in the world was Sam Patch?"

"Isabel, your ignorance of all that an American woman

should be proud of distresses me. Have you really, then, never heard of the man who invented the saying, 'Some things can be done as well as others,' and proved it by jumping over Niagara Falls twice? Spurred on by this belief, he attempted the leap of the Genesee Falls. The leap was easy enough, but the coming up again was another matter. He failed in that. It was the one thing that could not be done as well as others."

"Dreadful!" said Isabel, with the cheerfullest satisfaction. "But what has all that to do with Rochester?"

"Now, my dear! You don't mean to say you didn't know that the Genesee Falls were at Rochester? Upon my word, I'm ashamed. Why, we're within ten minutes' walk of them now."

"Then walk to them at once!" cried Isabel, wholly unabashed, and in fact unable to see what he had to be ashamed of. "Actually, I believe you would have allowed me to leave Rochester without telling me the Falls were here, if you hadn't happened to think of Sam Patch."

Saying this she persuaded herself that a chief object of their journey had been to visit the scene of Sam Patch's fatal exploit, and she drew Basil with a nervous swiftness in the direction of the railroad station, beyond which he said were the Falls. Presently, after threading their way among a multitude of locomotives, with and without trains attached, that backed and advanced, or stood still, hissing impatiently on every side, they passed through the station to a broad planking above the river on the other side, and thence, after encounter of more locomotives, they found, by dint of much asking, a street winding up the hill-side to the left, and leading to the German Bierhaus that gives access to the best view of the cataract.

The Americans have characteristically bordered the river with manufactures, making every drop work its passage to the brink; while the Germans have as characteristically made use of the beauty left over, and have built a Bierhaus where they may regale both soul and sense in the presence of the cataract. Our travellers might, in another mood and place, have thought it droll to arrive at that sublime spectacle through a Bierhaus, but in this enchanted city it seemed to have a peculiar fitness.

A narrow corridor gave into a wide festival space occupied by many tables, each of which was surrounded by a group of clamorous Germans of either sex and every age, with tall beakers of beaded lager before them, and slim flasks of Rhenish; overhead flamed the gas in globes of vari-coloured glass; the walls were painted like those of such haunts in the fatherland; and the wedding-journeyers were fain to linger on their way, to dwell upon that scene of honest enjoyment, to inhale the mingling odours of beer and of pipes, and of the pungent cheeses in which the children of the fatherland delight. Amidst the inspiriting clash of plates and glasses, the rattle of knives and forks, and the hoarse rush of gutturals, they could catch the words Franzosen, Kaiser, König, and Schlacht, and they knew that festive company to be exulting in the first German triumphs of the war, which were then the day's news; they saw fists shaken at noses in fierce exchange of joy, arms tossed abroad in wild congratulation, and health-pouring goblets of beer lifted in air. Then they stepped into the moonlight again, and heard only the solemn organ stops of the cataract. Through garden-ground they were led by the little maid, their guide, to a small pavilion, that stood on the edge of the precipitous shore, and commanded a perfect view of the Falls. As they entered this pavilion, a youth and maiden, clearly lovers, passed out, and they were left alone with that sublime presence. Something of definiteness was to be desired in the spectacle, but there was ample compensation in the mystery with which the broad effulgence and the dense unluminous shadows of the moonshine invested it. The light touched all the tops of the rapids, that seemed to writhe away from the brink of the cataract, and then desperately breaking and perishing to fall, the white disembodied ghosts of rapids, down to the bottom of the vast and deep ravine through which the river rushed away. Now the waters seemed to mass themselves a hundred feet high in a wall of snowy compactness, now to disperse into their multitudinous particles and hang like some vaporous cloud from the cliff. Every moment renewed the vision of beauty in some rare and fantastic shape; and its loveliness isolated it, in spite of the great town on the other shore, the station with its bridge and its trains, the mills that supplied their feeble little needs from the cataract's strength.

At last Basil pointed out the table-rock in the middle of the Fall, from which Sam Patch had made his fatal leap; but Isabel refused to admit that tragical figure to the honours of her emotions. "I don't care for him!" she said fiercely. "Patch! What a name to be linked in our thoughts with this superb cataract."

"Well, Isabel, I think you are very unjust. It's as good a name as Leander, to my thinking, and it was immortalized in support of a great idea,—the feasibility of all things; while Leander's has come down to us as that of the weak victim of a passion. We shall never have a poetry of our own till we get over this absurd reluctance from facts, till we make the ideal embrace and include the real, till we consent to face the music in our simple common names, and put Smith into a lyric and Jones into a tragedy. The Germans are braver than we, and in them you find facts and dreams continually blended and confronted. Here is a fortunate illustration. The people we met coming out of this pavilion were lovers, and they had been here sentimentalizing on this superb cataract, as you call it, with which my heroic Patch is not worthy to be named. No doubt they had been quoting Uhland or some other of their romantic poets, perhaps singing some of their tender German love-songs,—the tenderest, unearthliest love-songs in the world. At the same time they did not disdain the matter-of-fact corporeity in which their sentiment was enshrined; they fed it heartily and abundantly with the banquet whose relics we see here."

On a table before them stood a pair of beer-glasses, in the bottoms of which lurked scarce the foam of the generous liquor lately brimming them; some shreds of sausage, some rinds of Swiss cheese, bits of cold ham, crusts of bread, and the ashes of a pipe.

Isabel shuddered at the spectacle, but made no comment, and Basil went on; "Do you suppose *they* scorned the idea of Sam Patch as they gazed upon the Falls? On the contrary, I've no doubt that he recalled to her

the ballad which a poet of their language made about
him. It used to go the rounds of the German newspapers,
and I translated it, a long while ago, when I thought
that I too was in Arkadien geboren.

> " 'In the Bierhausgarten I linger
>   By the Falls of the Genesee:
> From the Table-Rock in the middle
>   Leaps a figure bold and free.
>
> " 'Aloof in the air it rises
>   O'er the rush, the plunge, the death;
> On the thronging banks of the river
>   There is neither pulse nor breath.
>
> " 'For ever it hovers and poises
>   Aloof in the moonlit air;
> As light as mist from the rapids,
>   As heavy as nightmare.
>
> " 'In anguish I cry to the people,
>   The long-since vanished hosts;
> I see them stretch forth in answer
>   The helpless hands of ghosts.'

I once met the poet who wrote this. He drank too much
beer."

"I don't see that he got in the name of Sam Patch,
after all," said Isabel.

"O yes, he did; but I had to yield to our taste, and
where he said, 'Springt der Sam Patsch kühn und frei,'
I made it 'Leaps a figure bold and free.' "

As they passed through the house on their way out,
they saw the youth and maiden they had met at the
pavilion door. They were seated at a table; two glasses
of beer towered before them; on their plates were odorous
crumbs of Limburger cheese. They both wore a pensive
air.

The next morning the illusion that had wrapt the whole earth was gone with the moonlight. By nine o'clock, when the wedding-journeyers resumed their way toward Niagara, the heat had already set in with the effect of ordinary midsummer's heat at high noon. The car into which they got had come the past night from Albany, and had an air of almost conscious shabbiness, griminess, and over-use. The seats were covered with cinders, which also crackled under foot. Dust was on everything, especially the persons of the crumpled and weary passengers of over-night. Those who came aboard at Rochester failed to lighten the spiritual gloom, and presently they sank into the common bodily wretchedness. The train was somewhat belated, and as it drew nearer Buffalo they knew the conductor to have abandoned himself to that blackest of the arts, making time. The long irregular jolt of the ordinary progress was reduced to an incessant shudder and a quick lateral motion. The air within the car was deadly; if a window was raised, a storm of dust and cinders blew in, and quick gusts caught away the breath. So they sat with closed windows, sweltering and stifling, and all the faces on which a lively horror was not painted were dull and damp with apathetic misery.

The incidents were in harmony with the abject physical tone of the company. There was a quarrel between a thin, shrill-voiced, highly dressed, much-bedizened Jewess, on the one side, and a fat, greedy old woman, half asleep, and a boy with large pink transparent ears that stood out from his head like the handles of a jar, on the other side, about a seat which the Hebrew wanted, and which the others had kept filled with packages on

G

the pretence that it was engaged. It was a loud and fierce quarrel enough, but it won no sort of favour; and when the Jewess had given a final opinion that the greedy old woman was no lady, and the boy, who disputed in an ironical temper, replied, "Highly complimentary, I *must* say," there was no sign of relief or other acknowledgment in any of the spectators, that there had been a quarrel.

There was a little more interest taken in the misfortune of an old purblind German and his son, who were found by the conductor to be a few hundred miles out of the direct course to their destination, and were with some trouble and the aid of an Americanized fellow countryman made aware of the fact. The old man then fell back in the prevailing apathy, and the child naturally cared nothing. By-and-by came the unsparing train-boy on his rounds, bestrewing the passengers successively with papers, magazines, fine-cut tobacco, and packages of candy. He gave the old man a package of candy, and passed on. The German took it as the bounty of the American people, oddly manifested in a situation where he could otherwise have had little proof of their care. He opened it, and was sharing it with his son when the train-boy came back, and metallically, like a part of the machinery, demanded, "Ten cents!" The German stared helplessly, and the boy repeated, "Ten cents! ten cents!" with tiresome patience, while the other passengers smiled. When it had passed through the alien's head that he was to pay for this national gift, and he took with his tremulous fingers from the recesses of his pocket-book a ten cent note and handed it to his tormentor, some of the people laughed. Among the rest, Basil and Isabel laughed, and then looked at each other with eyes of mutual reproach.

"Well, upon my word, my dear," he said, "I think we've fallen pretty low. I've never felt such a poor shabby ruffian before. Good heavens! To think of our immortal souls being moved to mirth by such a thing as this,—so stupid, so barren of all reason of laughter. And then the cruelty of it! What ferocious imbeciles we are! Whom have I married? A woman with neither heart nor brain!"

"O Basil, dear, pay him back the money—do."

"I can't. That's the worst of it. He's money enough, and might justly take offence. What breaks my heart is that we could have the depravity to smile at the mistake of a friendless stranger, who supposed he had at last met with an act of pure kindness. It's a thing to weep over. Look at these grinning wretches! What a fiendish effect their smiles have, through their cinders and sweat! O, it's the terrible weather; the despotism of the dust and heat; the wickedness of the infernal air. What a squalid and loathsome company!"

At Buffalo, where they arrived late, they found themselves with several hours' time on their hands before the train started for Niagara, and in the first moments of tedium, Isabel forgot herself into saying, "Don't you think we'd have done better to go directly from Rochester to the Falls, instead of coming this way?"

"Why certainly. I didn't propose coming this way."

"I know it, dear. I was only asking," said Isabel, meekly. "But I should think you'd have generosity enough to take a little of the blame, when I wanted to come out of a romantic feeling for you."

This romantic feeling referred to the fact that, many years before, when Basil made his first visit to Niagara, he had approached from the west by way of Buffalo; and Isabel, who tenderly begrudged his having existed before she knew him, and longed to ally herself retrospectively with his past, was resolved to draw near the great cataract by no other route.

She fetched a little sigh which might mean the weather or his hard-heartedness. The sigh touched him, and he suggested a carriage-ride through the city; she assented with eagerness, for it was what she had been thinking of. She had never seen a lake-side city before, and she was taken by surprise. "If ever we leave Boston," she said, "we will not live at Rochester, as I thought last night; we'll come to Buffalo." She found that the place had all the picturesqueness of a sea-port, without the ugliness that attends the rising and falling tides. A delicious freshness breathed from the lake, which lying so smooth, faded into the sky at last, with no line between sharper than that which divides drowsing from dreaming. But the colour was the most charming thing, that delicate blue of the lake, without the depth of the sea-blue, but infinitely softer and lovelier. The nearer expanses rippled with dainty waves, silver and lucent; the further levels made, with the sun-dimmed summer sky, a vague horizon of turquoise and amethyst, lit by the white sails of ships, and stained by the smoke of steamers.

"Take me away now," said Isabel, when her eyes had feasted upon all this, "and don't let me see another thing till I get to Niagara. Nothing less sublime is worthy the eyes that have beheld such beauty."

However, on the way to Niagara she consented to

glimpses of the river which carries the waters of the lake for their mighty plunge, and which shows itself very nobly from time to time as you draw toward the cataract, with wooded or cultivated islands, and rich farms along its low shores, and at last flashes upon the eye the shining white of the rapids,—a hint, no more, of the splendour and awfulness to be revealed.

VI.

A S the train stopped, Isabel's heart beat with a
child-like exultation, as I believe every one's
heart must who is worthy to arrive at Niagara.
She had been trying to fancy, from time to time, that
she heard the roar of the cataract, and now, when she
alighted from the car, she was sure she should have
heard it but for the vulgar little noises that attend the
arrival of trains at Niagara as well as everywhere else.
"Never mind, dearest; you shall be stunned with it before you leave," promised her husband; and, not wholly
disconsolate, she rode through the quaint streets of the
village, where it remains a question whether the lowliness
of the shops and private houses makes the hotels look so
vast, or the bigness of the hotels dwarfs all the other
buildings. The immense caravansaries swelling up from
among the little bazaars (where they sell feather fans,
and miniature bark canoes, and jars and vases and
bracelets and brooches carved out of the local rocks),
made our friends with their trunks very conscious of
their disproportion to the accommodations of the smallest.
They were the sole occupants of the omnibus, and they
were embarrassed to be received at their hotel with a
burst of minstrelsy from a whole band of music. Isabel
felt that a single stringed instrument of some timid note
would have been enough; and Basil was going to express

92

his own modest preference for a jew's-harp, when the
music ceased with a sudden clash of the cymbals. But
the next moment it burst out with fresh sweetness, and
in alighting they perceived that another omnibus had
turned the corner and was drawing up to the pillared
portico of the hotel. A small family dismounted, and
the feet of the last had hardly touched the pavement
when the music again ended as abruptly as those flour-
ishes of trumpets that usher player-kings upon the stage.
Isabel could not help laughing at this melodious parsi-
mony. "I hope they don't let on the cataract and shut
it off in this frugal style; do they, Basil?" she asked, and
passed jesting through a pomp of unoccupied porters and
call-boys. Apparently there were not many people stopping at this hotel, or else they were all out looking at the
Falls or confined to their rooms. However; our travellers took in the almost weird emptiness of the place with
their usual gratitude to fortune for all queerness in life,
and followed to the pleasant quarters assigned them.
There was time before supper for a glance at the cataract
and after a brief toilet they sallied out again upon the
holiday street, with its parade of gay little shops, and
thence passed into the grove beside the Falls, enjoying at
every instant their feeling of arrival at a sublime destination.

In this sense Niagara deserves almost to rank with
Rome, the metropolis of history and religion; with
Venice, the chief city of sentiment and fantasy. In
either you are at once made at home by a perception of its
greatness, in which there is no quality of aggression, as
there always seems to be in minor places as well as in
minor men, and you gratefully accept its sublimity as a
fact in no way contrasting with your own insignificance.

Our friends were beset of course by many carriage-drivers, whom they repelled with the kindly firmness of experienced travel. Isabel even felt a compassion for these poor fellows who had seen Niagara so much as to have forgotten that the first time one must see it alone or only with the next of friendship. She was voluble in her pity of Basil that it was not as new to him as to her, till between the trees they saw a white cloud of spray, shot through and through with sunset, rising, rising, and she felt her voice softly and steadily beaten down by the diapason of the cataract.

I am not sure but the first emotion on viewing Niagara is that of familiarity. Ever after, its strangeness increases; but in that earliest moment, when you stand by the side of the American Fall, and take in so much of the whole as your glance can compass, an impression of having seen it often before is certainly very vivid. This may be an effect of that grandeur which puts you at your ease in its presence; but it also undoubtedly results in part from lifelong acquaintance with every variety of futile picture of the scene. You have its outward form clearly in your memory; the shores, the rapids, the islands, the curve of the Falls, and the stout rainbow with one end resting on their top and the other lost in the mists that rise from the gulf beneath. On the whole I do not account this sort of familiarity a misfortune. The surprise is none the less a surprise because it is kept till the last, and the marvel, making itself finally felt in every nerve, and not at once through a single sense, all the more fully possesses you. It is as if Niagara reserved her magnificence, and preferred to win your

heart with her beauty; and so Isabel, who was in-
stinctively prepared for the reverse, suffered a vague
disappointment, for a little instant, as she looked along
the verge from the water that caressed the shore at her
feet before it flung itself down, to the wooded point that
divides the American from the Canadian Fall, beyond
which showed dimly through its veil of golden and silver
mists the emerald wall of the great Horse-Shoe. "How
still it is!" she said, amidst the roar that shook the
ground under their feet and made the leaves tremble
overhead, and "How lonesome!" amidst the people lounging and sauntering about in every direction among the
trees. In fact that prodigious presence does make a solitude and silence round every spirit worthy to perceive
it, and it gives a kind of dignity to all its belongings, so
that the rocks and pebbles in the water's edge, and the
weeds and grasses that nod above it, have a value far
beyond that of such common things elsewhere. In all
the aspects of Niagara there seems a grave simplicity
which is perhaps a reflection of the spectator's soul for
once utterly dismantled of affectation and convention.
In the vulgar reaction from this, you are of course as
trivial, if you like, at Niagara, as anywhere.

Slowly Isabel became aware that the sacred grove beside the Fall was profaned by some very common pres-
ences indeed, that tossed bits of stone and sticks into the
consecrated waters, and struggled for handkerchiefs and
fans, and here and there put their arms about each
other's waist, and made a show of laughing and joking.
They were a picnic party of rude, silly folks of the
neighbourhood, and she stood pondering them in sad
wonder if anything could be worse, when she heard a

voice saying to Basil, "Take you next, Sir? Plenty
of light yet, and the wind's down the river, so the
spray won't interfere. Make a capital picture of you;
Falls in the background." It was the local photographer
urging them to succeed the young couple he had
just posed at the brink: the gentleman was sitting down,
with his legs crossed and his hands elegantly disposed;
the lady was standing at his side, with one arm thrown
lightly across his shoulder, while with the other hand she
thrust his cane into the ground; you could see it was going to be a splendid photograph.

Basil thanked the artist, and Isabel said, trusting as
usual to his sympathy for perception of her train of
thought, "Well, I'll never try to be high-strung again.
But shouldn't you have thought, dearest, that I might
expect to be high-strung with success at Niagara if anywhere?" She passively followed him into the long, queer,
downward-sloping edifice on the border of the grove, un-
flinchingly mounted the car that stood ready, and descended the incline. Emerging into the light again,
she found herself at the foot of the Fall by whose top
she had just stood.

At first she was glad there were other people down
there, as if she and Basil were not enough to bear it
alone, and she could almost have spoken to the two
hopelessly pretty brides, with parasols and impertinent
little boots, whom their attendant husbands were helping
over the sharp and slippery rocks, so bare beyond the
spray, so green and mossy within the fall of mist. But
in another breath she forgot them as she looked on that
dizzied sea, hurling itself from the high summit in huge
white knots, and breaks and masses and plunging into

the gulf beside her, while it sent continually up a strong voice of lamentation, and crawled away in vast eddies, with somehow a look of human terror, bewilderment, and pain. It was bathed in snowy vapour to its crest, but now and then heavy currents of air drew this aside, and they saw the outline of the Falls almost as far as the Canada side. They remembered afterwards how they were able to make use of but one sense at a time, and how when they strove to take in the forms of the descending flood, they ceased to hear it; but as soon as they released their eyes from this service, every fibre in them vibrated to the sound, and the spectacle dissolved away in it. They were aware, too, of a strange capriciousness in their senses, and of a tendency of each to palter with the things perceived. The eye could no longer take truthful note of quality, and now beheld the tumbling deluge as a Gothic wall of cavern marble white, motionless, and now as a fall of lightest snow, with movement in all its atoms, and scarce so much cohesion as would hold them together; and again they could not discern if this course were from above or from beneath, whether the water rose from the abyss or dropped from the height. The ear could give the brain no assurance of the sound that filled it, and whether it were great or little; the prevailing softness of the cataract's tone seemed so much opposed to ideas of prodigious force or of prodigious volume. It was only when the sight, so idle in its own behalf, came to the aid of the other sense, and showed them the mute movement of each other's lips, that they dimly appreciated the depth of sound that involved them.

"I think you might have been high-strung there, for a second or two," said Basil, when, ascending the incline, he could make himself heard. "We will try the bridge next."

Over the river, so still with its oily eddies and delicate wreaths of foam, just below the Falls they have in late years woven a web of wire high in air, and hung a bridge from precipice to precipice. Of all the bridges made with hands it seems the lightest, most ethereal; it is ideally graceful, and droops from its slight towers like a garland. It is worthy to command, as it does, the whole grandeur of Niagara, and to show the traveller the vast spectacle from the beginning of the American Fall to the furthest limit of the Horse-Shoe, with all the awful pomp of the rapids, the solemn darkness of the wooded islands, the mystery of the vaporous gulf, the indomitable wildness of the shores, as far as the eye can reach up or down the fatal stream.

To this bridge our friends now repaired, by a path that led through another of those groves which keep the village back from the shores of the river on the American side, and greatly help the sight-seer's pleasure in the place. The exquisite structure, which sways so tremulously from its towers, and seems to lay so slight a hold on earth where its cables sink into the ground, is to other bridges what the blood horse is to the common breed of roadsters; and now they felt its sensitive nerves quiver under them and sympathetically through them as they advanced further and further toward the centre. Perhaps their sympathy with the bridge's trepidation was too great for unalloyed delight, and yet the thrill was a glorious one to be known only there; and afterwards, at least, they would not have had their airy path seem more secure.

The last hues of sunset lingered in the mists that sprung from the base of the Falls with a mournful, tremulous grace, and a movement weird as the play of the northern lights. They were touched with the most delicate purples and crimsons, that darkened to deep red, and then faded from them at a second look, and then flew upward, swiftly upward, like troops of pale, transparent ghosts; while a perfectly clear radiance, better than any other for local colour, dwelt upon the scene. Far under the bridge the river smoothly swam, the under-currents for ever unfolding themselves upon the surface with a vast rose-like evolution, edged all round with faint lines of white, where the air that filled the water freed itself in foam. What had been clear green on the face of the cataract was here more like rich verd-antique, and had a look of firmness almost like that of the stone itself. So it showed beneath the bridge, and down the river till the curving shores hid it. These, springing abruptly from the water's brink, and shagged with pine and cedar, displayed the tender verdure of grass and bushes intermingled with the dark evergreens that climb from ledge to ledge, till they point their speary tops above the crest of bluffs. In front, where tumbled rocks and expanses of naked clay varied the gloomier and gayer green, sprung those spectral mists; and through them loomed out, in its manifold majesty, Niagara, with the seemingly immovable white Gothic screen of the American Fall, and the green massive curve of the Horse-Shoe, solid and simple and calm as an Egyptian wall; while behind this, with their white and black expanses broken by dark-foliaged

little isles, the steep Canadian rapids billowed down between their heavily wooded shores.

The wedding-journeyers hung, they know not how
long, in rapture on the sight; and then, looking back
from the shore to the spot where they had stood, they
felt relieved that unreality should possess itself of all,
and that the bridge should swing there in mid-air like a
filmy web, scarce more passable than the rainbow that
flings its arch above the mists.

On the portico of the hotel they found half a score of
gentlemen smoking and creating together that collective
silence which passes for sociality on our continent. Some
carriages stood before the door, and within, around the
base of a pillar sat a circle of idle call-boys. There were
a few trunks heaped together in one place, with a porter
standing guard over them; a solitary guest was buying a
cigar at the newspaper stand in one corner; another
friendless creature was writing a letter in the reading-
room; the clerk, in a seersucker coat and a lavish shirt-
bosom, tried to give the whole an effect of watering-place
gaiety and bustle, as he provided a newly arrived guest
with a room.

Our pair took in these traits of solitude and repose
with indifference. If the hotel had been thronged with
brilliant company, they would have been no more and no
less pleased; and when, after supper, they came into the
grand parlour, and found nothing there but a marble-
topped centre-table, with a silver-plated ice-pitcher and
a small company of goblets, they sat down perfectly content in a secluded window-seat. They were not seen
by the three people who entered soon after, and halted
in the centre of the room.

"Why, Kitty!" said one of the two ladies who must be in any travelling-party of three, "this is more inappropriate to your gorgeous array than the supper-room, even."

She who was called Kitty was armed, as for social conquest, in some kind of airy evening-dress, and was looking round with bewilderment upon that forlorn waste of carpeting and upholstery. She owned, with a smile, that she had not seen so much of the world yet as she had been promised; but she liked Niagara very much, and perhaps they should find the world at breakfast.

"No," said the other lady, who was as unquiet as Kitty was calm, and who seemed resolved to make the most of the worst, "it isn't probable that the hotel will fill up overnight; and I feel personally responsible for this state of things. Who would ever have supposed that Niagara would be so empty? I thought the place was thronged the whole summer long. How do you account for it, Richard?"

The gentleman looked fatigued, as from a long-continued discussion elsewhere of the matter in hand, and he said that he had not been trying to account for it.

Then you don't care for Kitty's pleasure at all, and you don't want her to enjoy herself. Why don't you take some interest in the matter?"

"Why, if I accounted for the emptiness of Niagara in the most satisfactory way, it wouldn't add a soul to the floating population. Under the circumstances I prefer to leave it unexplained."

"Do you think it's because it's such a hot summer? Do you suppose it's not exactly the season? Didn't you expect there'd be more people? Perhaps Niagara isn't as fashionable as it used to be."

"It looks something like that."

"Well, what under the sun do you think *is* the reason?"

"I don't know."

"Perhaps," interposed Kitty, placidly, "most of the visitors go to the other hotel, now."

"It's altogether likely," said the other lady, eagerly. "There are just such caprices."

"Well," said Richard, "I wanted you to go there."

"But you said that you always heard this was the most fashionable."

"I know it. I didn't want to come here for that reason. But fortune favours the brave."

"Well, it's too bad! Here we've asked Kitty to come to Niagara with us, just to give her a little peep into the world, and you've brought us to a hotel where we're"—

"'Monarchs of all we survey,'" suggested Kitty.

"Yes, 'and start at the sound of our own,'" added the other lady, helplessly.

"Come now, Fanny," said the gentleman, who was but too clearly the husband of the last speaker. "You know you insisted, against all I could say or do, upon coming to this house; I implored you to go to the other, and now you blame me for bringing you here."

"So I do. If you'd let me have my own way without opposition about coming here, I dare say I should have gone to the other place. But never mind. Kitty knows whom to blame, I hope. She's *your* cousin."

Kitty was sitting with her hands quiescently folded in her lap. She now rose and said that she did not know anything about the other hotel, and perhaps it was just as empty as this.

"It can't be. There can't be *two* hotels so empty," said Fanny. "It don't stand to reason."

"If you wish Kitty to see the world so much," said the gentleman, "why don't you take her on to Quebec, with us?"

Kitty had left her seat beside Fanny, and was moving with a listless content about the parlour.

"I wonder you ask, Richard, when you know she's only come for the night, and has nothing with her but a few cuffs and collars! I certainly never heard of anything so absurd before!"

The absurdity of the idea then seemed to cast its charm upon her, for, after a silence, "I could lend her some things," she said musingly. "But don't speak of it to-night, please. It's *too* ridiculous. Kitty!" she called out, and, as the young lady drew near, she continued, "How would you like to go to Quebec, with us?"

"O Fanny!" cried Kitty, with rapture; and then, with dismay, "How *can* I?"

"Why, very well, I think. You've got this dress, and your travelling suit; and I can lend you whatever you want. Come!" she added joyously, "let's go up to your room, and talk it over!"

The two ladies vanished upon this impulse, and the gentleman followed. To their own relief the guiltless eaves-droppers, who found no moment favourable for revealing themselves after the comedy began, issued from their retiracy.

"What a remarkable little lady!" said Basil, eagerly

H

turning to Isabel for sympathy in his enjoyment of her inconsequence.

"Yes, poor thing!" returned his wife; "it's no light matter to invite a young lady to take a journey with you, and promise her all sorts of gaiety, and perhaps beaux and flirtations, and then find her on your hands in a desolation like this. It's dreadful, I think."

Basil stared. "O certainly," he said. "But what an amusingly illogical little body!"

"I don't understand what you mean, Basil. It was the only thing that she could do, to invite the young lady to go on with them. I wonder her husband had the sense to think of it first. Of *course* she'll have to lend her things."

"And you didn't observe anything peculiar in her way of reaching her conclusions?"

"Peculiar? What *do* you mean?"

"Why, her blaming her husband for letting her have her own way about the hotel; and her telling him not to mention his proposal to Kitty, and then doing it herself, just after she'd pronounced it absurd and impossible." He spoke with heat at being forced to make what he thought a needless explanation.

"O!" said Isabel, after a moment's reflection. *"That!"* Did you think it so very odd?"

Her husband looked at her with the gravity a man must feel when he begins to perceive that he has married the whole mystifying world of womankind in the woman of his choice, and made no answer. But to his own soul he said: "I supposed I had the pleasure of my wife's acquaintance. It seems I have been flattering myself."

The next morning they went out as they had planned,
for an exploration of Goat Island, after an early breakfast. As they sauntered through the village's contrasts
of pigmy and colossal in architecture, they praisefully
took in the unalloyed holiday character of the place, enjoying equally the lounging tourists at the hotel doors,
the drivers and their carriages to let, and the little shops,
with nothing but mementos of Niagara, and Indian
beadwork, and other trumpery, to sell. Shops so useless, they agreed, could not be found outside the Palais
Royal, or the Square of St. Mark, or anywhere else in the
world but here. They felt themselves once more a part
of the tide of mere sight-seeing pleasure-travel, on which
they had drifted in other days, and in an eddy of which
their love itself had opened its white blossom, and lily-
like dreamed upon the wave.

They were now also part of the great circle of newly
wedded bliss, which, involving the whole land during the
season of bridal tours, may be said to show richest and
fairest at Niagara, like the costly jewel of a precious ring.
The place is, in fact, almost abandoned to bridal couples,
and any one out of his honey-moon is in some degree an
alien there, and must discern a certain immodesty in his
intrusion. Is it for his profane eyes to look upon all
that blushing and trembling joy? A man of any
sensibility must desire to veil his face, and, bowing his
excuses to the collective rapture, take the first train for
the wicked outside world to which he belongs. Everywhere, he sees brides and brides. Three or four with
the benediction still on them, come down in the same
car with him; he hands her travelling-shawl after one
as she springs from the omnibus into her husband's

arms; there are two or three walking back and forth
with their new lords upon the porch of the hotel; at
supper they are on every side of him, and he feels himself suffused, as it were, by a roseate atmosphere of
youth and love and hope. At breakfast it is the same,
and then, in his wanderings about the place he constantly
meets them. They are of all manners of beauty, fair and
dark, slender and plump, tall and short; but they are all
beautiful with the radiance of loving and being loved.
Now, if ever in their lives, they are charmingly dressed,
and ravishing toilets take the willing eye from the objects
of interest. How high the heels of the pretty boots, how
small the tender-tinted gloves, how electrical the flutter
of the snowy skirts! What is Niagara to these things?

Isabel was not willing to own her bridal sisterhood to
these blessed souls; but she secretly rejoiced in it, even
while she joined Basil in noting their number and smiling at their innocent abandon. She dropped his arm at
encounter of the first couple, and walked carelessly at
his side; she made a solemn vow never to take hold of his
watch-chain in speaking to him; she trusted that she
might be preserved from putting her face very close to
his at dinner in studying the bill of fare; getting out of
carriages, she forbade him ever to take her by the waist.
All ascetic resolutions are modified by experiment; but if
Isabel did not rigorously keep these, she is not the less
to be praised for having formed them.

Just before they reached the bridge to Goat Island,
they passed a little group of the Indians still lingering
about Niagara, who make the barbaric wares in which
the shops abound, and, like the woods and the wild faces
of the cliffs and precipices, help to keep the cataract

remote, and to invest it with the charm of primeval lone-
liness. This group were women, and they sat motionless
on the ground, smiling sphinx-like over their laps full of
bead-work, and turning their dark liquid eyes of invi-
tation upon the passers. They wore bright kirtles, and
red shawls fell from their heads over their plump brown
cheeks and down their comfortable persons. A little girl
with them was attired in like gaiety of colour. "What
is her name?" asked Isabel, paying for a bead pincushion.
"Daisy Smith," said her mother, in distressingly good
English. "But her Indian name?" "She has none,"
answered the woman, who told Basil that her village
numbered five hundred people, and that they were
Protestants. While they talked they were joined by an
Indian, whom the women saluted musically in their
native tongue. This was somewhat consoling; but he
wore trousers and a waistcoat, and it could have been
wished that he had not a silk hat on.

"Still," said Isabel, as they turned away, "I'm glad he
hasn't Lisle-thread gloves, like that chieftain we saw
putting his forest queen on board the train at Oneida.
But how shocking that they should be Christians, and
Protestants! It would have been bad enough to have them
Catholics. And that woman said that they were increasing. They ought to be fading away."

On the bridge, they paused and looked up and down
the rapids rushing down the slope in all their wild
variety, with the white crests of breaking surf, the dark
massiveness of heavy-climbing waves, the fleet, smooth
sweep of currents over broad shelves of sunken rock, the
dizzy swirl and suck of whirlpools.

Spell-bound, the journeyers pored upon the deathful

course beneath their feet, gave a shudder to the horror of being cast upon it, and then hurried over the bridge to the island, in the shadow of whose wildness they sought refuge from the sight and sound.

There had been rain in the night; the air was full of forest fragrance, and the low, sweet voice of twittering birds. Presently they came to a bench set in a corner of the path, and commanding a pleasant vista of sunlit foliage, with a mere gleam of the foaming river beyond. As they sat down here loverwise, Basil, as in the early days of their courtship, began to recite a poem. It was one which had been haunting him since his first sight of the rapids, one of many that he used to learn by heart in his youth—the rhyme of some poor newspaper poet, whom the third or fourth editor copying his verses consigned to oblivion by carelessly clipping his name from the bottom. It had always lingered in Basil's memory, rather from the interest of the awful fact it recorded, than from any merit of its own; and now he recalled it with a distinctness that surprised him.

AVERY.

I.

All night long they heard in the houses beside the shore,
Heard, or seemed to hear, through the multitudinous roar,
Out of the hell of the rapids as 'twere a lost soul's cries:
Heard and could not believe; and the morning mocked their eyes,
Showing, where wildest and fiercest the waters leaped up and ran
Raving round him and past, the visage of a man
Clinging, or seeming to cling, to the trunk of a tree that, caught
Fast in the rocks below, scarce out of the surges raught.
Was it a life, could it be, to yon slender hope that clung?
Shrill, above all the tumult the answering terror rung.

II.

Under the weltering rapids a boat from the bridge is drowned,
Over the rocks the lines of another are tangled and wound,
And the long, fateful hours of the morning have wasted soon,
As it had been in some blessed trance, and now it is noon.
Hurry, now with the raft! But O, build it strong and stanch,
And to the lines and the treacherous rocks look well as you
      launch
Over the foamy tops of the waves, and their foam-sprent sides,
Over the hidden reefs, and through the embattled tides,
Onward rushes the raft, with many a lurch and leap,—
Lord! if it strike him loose from the hold he scarce can keep!
No! through all peril unharmed, it reaches him harmless at last,
And to its proven strength he lashes his weakness fast.
Now, for the shore! But steady, steady, my men, and slow;
Taut, now, the quivering lines; now slack; and so, let her go!
Thronging the shores around stands the pitying multitude;
Wan as his own are their looks, and a nightmare seems to brood
Heavy upon them, and heavy the silence hangs on all,
Save for the rapids' plunge, and the thunder of the Fall.
But on a sudden thrills from the people still and pale,
Chorussing his unheard despair, a desperate wail;
Caught on a lurking point of rock it sways and swings,
Sport of the pitiless waters, the raft to which he clings.

III.

All the long afternoon it idly swings and sways;
And on the shore the crowd lifts up its hands and prays:
Lifts to heaven and wrings the hands so helpless to save,
Prays for the mercy of God on him whom the rock and the
      wave
Battle for, fettered betwixt them, and who amidst their strife
Struggles to help his helpers, and fights so hard for his life,—
Tugging at rope and at reef, while men weep and women swoon.
Priceless second by second, so wastes the afternoon.
And it is sunset now; and another boat and the last
Down to him from the bridge through the rapids has safely
      passed.

IV.

Wild through the crowd comes flying a man that nothing can
      stay
Maddening against the gate that is locked athwart his way.

"No! we keep the bridge for them that can help him. You,
Tell us, who are you?" "His brother!" "God help you both!
        Pass through."
And from the bridge he sees his brother sever the rope
Wild, with wide arms of imploring he calls aloud to him,
Unto the face of his brother, scarce seen in the distance dim;
But in the roar of the rapids his fluttering words are lost
As in a wind of autumn the leaves of autumn are tossed.
Holding him to the raft, and rises secure in his hope;
Sees all as in a dream the terrible pageantry,—
Populous shores, the woods, the sky, the birds flying free;
Sees, then, the form—that, spent with effort and fasting and
        fear,
Flings itself feebly and fails of the boat that is lying so near,—
Caught in the long-baffled clutch of the rapids, and rolled and
        hurled
Headlong on to the cataract's brink, and out of the world.

"O Basil!" said Isabel, with a long sigh breaking the
hush that best praised the unknown poet's skill, "it *isn't*
true, is it?"

"Every word, almost, even to the brother's coming at
the last moment. It's a very well known incident," he
added, and I am sure the reader whose memory runs
back twenty years cannot have forgotten it.

Niagara, indeed, is an awful homicide; nearly every
point of interest about the place has killed its man, and
there might well be a deeper stain of crimson than it
ever wears in that pretty bow over-arching the Falls. Its
beauty is relieved against an historical background as
gloomy as the lightest-hearted tourist could desire. The
abominable savages, revering the cataract as a kind of
august devil, and leading a life of demoniacal misery and
wickedness, whom the first Jesuits found here two
hundred years ago; the ferocious Iroquois bloodily driving out these squalid devil-worshippers; the French
planting the fort that yet guards the mouth of the river,

and therewith the seeds of war that fruited afterwards
in murderous strife throughout the whole Niagara
country; the struggle for the military posts on the river,
during the wars of France and England; the awful scene
in the conspiracy of Pontiac, where a detachment of
English troops was driven by the Indians over the
precipice near the great whirlpool; the sorrow and havoc
visited upon the American settlements in the Revolution
by the savages who prepared their attacks in the shadow
of Fort Niagara; the battles of Chippewa and of Lundy's
Lane, that mixed the roar of their cannon with that of
the Fall; the savage forays with tomahawk and scalping-
knife, and the blazing villages on either shore in the War
of 1812,—these are the memories of the place, the links
in a chain of tragical interest scarcely broken before our
time since the white man first beheld the mist-veiled face
of Niagara. The facts lost nothing of their due effect as
Basil, in the ramble across Goat Island, touched them
with the reflected light of Mr. Parkman's histories,—
those precious books that make our meagre past wear
something of the rich romance of old European days, and
illumine its savage solitudes with the splendour of
mediæval chivalry, and the glory of mediæval martyrdom,—and then, lacking this light, turned upon them
the feeble glimmer of the guide-books. He and Isabel
enjoyed the lurid picture with all the zest of sentimentalists dwelling upon the troubles of other times from
the shelter of the safe and peaceful present. They were
both poets in their quality of bridal couple, and so long
as their own nerves were unshaken they could transmute
all facts to entertaining fables. They pleasantly exercised their sympathies upon those who every year perish

at Niagara in the tradition of its awful power; only they refused their cheap and selfish compassion to the Hermit of Goat Island, who dwelt so many years in its conspicuous seclusion, and was finally carried over the cataract. This public character they suspected of design in his death as in his life, and they would not be moved by his memory; though they gave a sigh to that dream, half pathetic, half ludicrous, yet not ignoble, of Mordecai Noah, who thought to assemble all the Jews of the world, and all the Indians, as remnants of the lost tribes, upon Grand Island, there to re-build Jerusalem, and who actually laid the cornerstone of the new temple there.

Goat Island is marvellously wild for a place visited by so many thousands every year. The shrubbery and undergrowth remain unravaged, and form a deceitful privacy, in which, even at that early hour of the day, they met many other pairs. It seemed incredible that the village and the hotels should be so full, and that the wilderness should also abound in them; yet on every embowered seat, and going to and from all points of interest and danger, were these new-wedded lovers with their interlacing arms and their fond attitudes, in which each seemed to support and lean upon the other. Such a pair stood prominent before them when Basil and Isabel emerged at last from the cover of the woods at the head of the island, and glanced up the broad swift stream to the point where it ran smooth before breaking into the rapids; and as a soft pastoral feature in the foreground of that magnificent landscape, they found them far from unpleasing. Some such pair is in the foreground of every famous American landscape; and when I think of the amount of public love-making in the season of pleasure-travel, from Mount Desert to the Yosemite, and from the parks of Colorado to the Keys of Florida, I feel that our continent is but a larger Arcady, that the middle of the nineteenth century is the golden age, and that we want very little of being a nation of shepherds and shepherdesses.

Our friends returned by the shore of the Canadian rapids, having traversed the island by a path through the heart of the woods, and now drew slowly near the Falls again. All parts of the prodigious pageant have an eternal novelty, and they beheld the ever-varying effect of that constant sublimity with the sense of discoverers, or rather of people whose great fortune it is to see the marvel in its beginning, and new from the creating hand. The morning hour lent its sunny charm to this illusion, while in the cavernous precipices of the shores, dark with evergreens, a mystery as of primeval night seemed to linger. There was a wild fluttering of their nerves, a rapture with an underconsciousness of pain, the exultation of peril and escape, when they came to the three little isles that extended from Goat Island, one beyond another far out into the furious channel. Three pretty suspension-bridges connect them now with the larger island, and under each of these flounders a huge rapid, and hurls itself away to mingle with the ruin of the fall. The Three Sisters are mere fragments of wilderness, clumps of vine-tangled woods, planted upon masses of rock; but they are part of the fascination of Niagara which no one resists; nor could Isabel have been persuaded from exploring them. It wants no courage to do this, but merely submission to the local sorcery, and the adventurer has no other reward than the consciousness of having been where but a few years before no human being had perhaps set foot. She crossed from bridge to bridge with a quaking heart, and at last stood upon the outermost isle, whence, through the screen of vines and boughs, she gave fearful glances at the heaving and tossing flood beyond, from every wave of which at every instant she rescued herself with a desperate struggle. The exertion told heavily upon her strength unawares, and she suddenly made Basil another revelation of character. Without the slightest warning she sank down at the root of a tree, and said, with serious composure that she could never go back on those bridges; they were not safe. He stared at her cowering form in blank amaze, and put his hands in his pockets. Then it occurred to his dull masculine sense that it must be a joke; and he said, "Well, I'll have you taken off in a boat."

"O *do*, Basil, *do*, have me taken off in a boat!" implored Isabel. "You see yourself the bridges are not safe. *Do* get a boat."

"Or a balloon," he suggested, humouring the pleasantry.

Isabel burst into tears; and now he went on his knees at her side and took her hands in his. "Isabel! Isabel! Are you crazy?" he cried, as if he meant to go mad himself. She moaned and shuddered in reply; he said, to mend matters, that it was a jest, about the boat; and he was driven to despair when Isabel repeated, "I never can go back by the bridges, never."

"But what do you propose to do?"

"I don't know, I don't know!"

He would try sarcasm. "Do you intend to set up a

hermitage here, and have your meals sent out from the hotel? It's a charming spot, and visited pretty constantly; but it's small even for a hermitage."

Isabel moaned again with her hands still on her eyes, and wondered that he was not ashamed to make fun of her.

He would try kindness. "Perhaps, darling, you'll let me carry you ashore."

"No, that will bring double the weight on the bridge at once."

"Couldn't you shut your eyes, and let me lead you?"

"Why, it isn't the *sight* of the rapids," she said, looking up fiercely. *"The bridges are not safe.* I'm not a *child,* Basil. O, *what* shall we do?"

"I don't know," said Basil, gloomily. "It's an exigency for which I wasn't prepared." Then he silently gave himself to the Evil One, for having probably overwrought Isabel's nerves by repeating that poem about Avery, and by the ensuing talk about Niagara, which she had seemed to enjoy so much. He asked her if that was it; and she answered, "Oh no, it's nothing but the bridges." He proved to her that the bridges, upon all known principles, were perfectly safe, and that they could not give way. She shook her head, but made no answer, and he lost his patience.

"Isabel" he cried, "I'm ashamed of you!"

"Don't say anything you'll be sorry for afterwards, Basil," she replied, with the forbearance of those who have reason and justice on their side.

The rapids beat and shouted round their little prison-isle, each billow leaping as if possessed by a separate demon. The absurd horror of the situation overwhelmed him. He dared not attempt to carry her ashore, for she might spring from his grasp into the flood. He could not leave her to call for help; and what if nobody came till she lost her mind from terror? Or, what if somebody should come and find them in that ridiculous affliction?

Somebody *was* coming!

"Isabel!" he shouted in her ear, "here come those people we saw in the parlour last night."

Isabel dashed her veil over her face, clutched Basil's with her icy hand, rose, drew her arm convulsively through his, and walked ashore without a word.

In a sheltered nook they sat down, and she quickly "repaired her drooping head and tricked her beams" again. He could see her tearfully smiling through her veil. "My dear," he said, "I don't ask an explanation of your fright, for I don't suppose you could give it. But should you mind telling me why those people were so sovereign against it?"

"Why, dearest! Don't you understand? That Mrs. Richard—whoever she is—is so much like *me*."

She looked at him as if she had made the most satisfying statement, and he thought he had better not ask further then, but wait in hope that the meaning would come to him. They walked on in silence till they came to the Biddle Stairs, at the head of which is a notice that persons have been killed by pieces of rock from the precipice overhanging the shore below, and warning people that they descend at their peril. Isabel declined to visit the Cave of the Winds, to which these stairs lead, but was willing to risk the ascent of Terrapin Tower. "Thanks; no," said her husband. "You might find it

unsafe to come back the way you went up. We can't
count certainly upon the appearance of the lady who is
so much like you; and I've no fancy for spending my
life on Terrapin Tower." So he found her a seat, and
went alone to the top of the audacious little structure
standing on the verge of the cataract, between the
smooth curve of the Horse-Shoe and the sculptured front
of the Central Fall, with the stormy sea of the rapids
behind, and the river, dimly seen through the mists,
crawling away between its lofty bluffs before. He knew
again the awful delight with which so long ago he had
watched the changes in the beauty of the Canadian Fall
as it hung a mass of translucent green from the brink,
and a pearly white seemed to crawl up from the abyss,
and penetrate all its substance to the very crest, and then
suddenly vanished from it, and perpetually renewed
the same effect. The mystery of the rising vapours veiled
the gulf into which the cataract swooped; the sun shone,
and a rainbow dreamed upon them.

Near the foot of the tower, some loose rocks extend
quite to the verge, and here Basil saw an elderly gentleman skipping from one slippery stone to another, and
looking down from time to time into the abyss, who,
when he had amused himself long enough in this way,
clambered up on the plank bridge. Basil, who had descended by this time, made bold to say that he thought
the diversion an odd one and rather dangerous. The
gentleman took this in good part, and owned it might
seem so, but added that a distinguished phrenologist had
examined his head, and told him he had equilibrium so
large that he could go anywhere.

"On your bridal tour, I presume," he continued, as

they approached the bench where Basil had left Isabel. She had now the company of a plain, middle-aged woman, whose attire hesitatingly expressed some inward festivity, and had a certain reluctant fashionableness. "Well, this is my third bridal tour to Niagara, and wife's been here once before on the same business. We see a good many changes. I used to stand on Table Rock with the others. Now that's *all* gone. Well, old lady, shall we move on?" he asked; and this bridal pair passed up the path, attended, happily, by the guardian spirits of those who gave the place so many sad yet pleasing associations.

At dinner, Mr. Richard's party sat the table next Basil's, and they were all now talking cheerfully over the emptiness of the spacious dining-hall.

"Well, Kitty," the married lady was saying, "you can tell the girls what you please about the gaieties of Niagara, when you get home. They'll believe anything sooner than the truth."

"O yes, indeed," said Kitty, "I've got a good deal of it made up already. I'll describe a grand hop at the hotel, with fashionable people from all parts of the country, and the gentlemen I danced with the most. I'm going to have had quite a flirtation with the gentleman of the long blonde moustache, whom we met on the bridge this morning, and he's got to do duty in accounting for my missing glove. It'll never do to tell the girls I dropped it from the top of Terrapin Tower. Then you know, Fanny, I really *can* say something about dining with aristocratic Southerners, waited upon by their black servants."

This referred to the sad-faced patrician whom Basil

and Isabel had noted in the cars from Buffalo as a Southerner probably coming North for the first time since the war. He had an air at once fierce and sad, and a half-barbaric, homicidal gentility of manner fascinating enough in its way. He sat with his wife at a table further down the room, and their child was served in part by a little tan-coloured nurse-maid. The fact did not quite answer to the young lady's description of it, and yet it certainly afforded her a ground-work. Basil fancied a sort of bewilderment in the Southerner, and explained it upon the theory that he used to come every year to Niagara before the war, and was now puzzled to find it so changed.

"Yes," he said, "I can't account for him except as the ghost of Southern travel, and I can't help feeling a little sorry for him. I suppose that almost any evil commends itself by its ruin; the wrecks of slavery are fast growing a fungus crop of sentiment, and they may yet outflourish the remains of the feudal system in the kind of poetry they produce. The impoverished slave-holder *is* a pathetic figure, in spite of all justice and reason; the beaten rebel *does* move us to compassion, and it is no use to think of Andersonville in his presence. This gentleman, and others like him, used to be the lords of our summer resorts. They spent the money they did not earn like princes; they held their heads high; they trampled upon the Abolitionist in his lair; they received the homage of the doughface in his home. They came up here from their rice-swamps and cotton-fields, and bullied the whole busy civilization of the North. Everybody who had merchandise of principles to sell truckled to them, and travel amongst us was a triumphal

I

progress. Now they're moneyless and subjected (as they call it), there's none so poor to do them reverence, and it's left for me, an Abolitionist from the cradle, to sigh over their fate. After all, they had noble traits, and it was no great wonder they got to despise us, seeing what most of us were. It seems to me I should like to know our friend. I can't help feeling towards him as towards a fallen prince, heaven help my craven spirit! I wonder how our colored waiter feels towards him. I dare say he admires him immensely."

There were not above a dozen other people in the room, and Basil contrasted the scene with that which the same formerly presented. "In the old time," he said, "every table was full, and we dined to the music of a brass band. I can't say I liked the band, but I miss it. I wonder if our Southern friend misses it? They gave us a very small allowance of brass band when we arrived, Isabel. Upon my word, I wonder what's come over the place," he said, as the Southern party, rising from the table, walked out of the dining-room, attended by many treacherous echoes in spite of an ostentatious clatter of dishes that the waiters made.

After dinner they drove on the Canada shore up past the Clifton House, towards the Burning Springs, which is not the least wonder of Niagara. As each bubble breaks upon the troubled surface, and yields its flash of infernal flame and its whiff of sulphurous stench, it seems hardly strange that the Neutral Nation should have revered the cataract as a demon; and another subtle spell (not to be broken even by the business-like composure of the man who shows off the hell-broth) is added to those successive sorceries by which Niagara gradually changes from a thing of beauty to a thing of terror. By all odds, too, the most tremendous view of the Falls is afforded by the point on this drive whence you look down upon the Horse-Shoe, and behold its three massive walls of sea rounding and sweeping into the gulf together, the colour gone, and the smooth brink showing black and ridgy.

Would they not go to the battle-field of Lundy's Lane? asked the driver at a certain point on their return; but Isabel did not care for battle-fields, and Basil preferred to keep intact the reminiscence of his former visit. "They have a sort of tower of observation built on the battle-ground," he said, as they drove on down by the river, "and it was in charge of an old Canadian militia-man, who had helped his countrymen to be beaten in the fight. This hero gave me a simple and unintelligible account of the battle, asking me first if I had ever heard of General Scott, and adding without flinching that here he got his earliest laurels. He seemed to go just so long to every listener, and nothing could stop him short, so I fell into a reverie until he came to an end. It was hard to remember, that sweet summer morning, when the sun shone, and the birds sang, and the music of a piano and girl's voice rose from a bowery cottage near, that all the pure air had once been tainted with battle-smoke, that the peaceful fields had been planted with cannon, instead of potatoes and corn, and that where the cows came down the farmer's lane, with tinkling bells, the shock of armed men had befallen. The blue and tranquil Ontario gleamed far away, and far away rolled the beautiful land, with farm-houses, fields, and woods, and at the foot of the tower lay the pretty village. The battle of the past seemed only a vagary of mine; yet how could I doubt the warrior at my elbow?—grieved though I was to find that a habit of strong drink had the better of his utterance that morning. My driver explained afterwards, that persons visiting the field were commonly so much pleased with the captain's eloquence, that they kept the noble old soldier in a brandy-and-water rapture throughout the season, thereby greatly refreshing his memory, and making the battle bloodier and bloodier as the season advanced and the number of visitors increased. "There my dear," he suddenly broke off, as they came in sight of a slender stream of water that escaped from the brow of a cliff on the American side below the Falls, and spun itself into a gauze of silvery mist, "that's the Bridal Veil; and I suppose you think the stream, which is making such a fine display, yonder, is some idle brooklet, ending a long course of error and worthlessness by that spectacular plunge. It's nothing of the kind; it's an honest hydraulic canal, of the most straightforward character, a poor but respectable mill-race which has devoted itself strictly to business, and has turned mill-wheels instead of fooling round water-lilies. It can afford that ultimate finery. What you behold in the Bridal Veil, my love, is the apotheosis of industry."

"What I can't help thinking of," said Isabel, who had not paid the smallest attention to the Bridal Veil, or anything about it "is the awfulness of stepping off these places in the night-time." She referred to the road which, next the precipice, is unguarded by any sort of parapet. In Europe a strong wall would secure it, but we manage things differently on our continent, and carriages go ruining over the brink from time to time.

"If your thoughts have that direction," answered her husband, "we had better go back to the hotel, and leave the Whirlpool for to-morrow morning. It's late for it to-day, at any rate." He had treated Isabel since the adventure on the Three Sisters with a superiority which he felt himself to be very odious, but which he could not disuse.

"I'm not afraid," she sighed, "but in the words of the retreating soldier, 'I'm awfully demoralized;'" and added, "You know we must reserve some of the vital forces for shopping this evening."

Part of their business also was to buy the tickets for their return to Boston by way of Montreal and Quebec, and it was part of their pleasure to get these of the heartiest imaginable ticket-agent. He was a colonel or at least a major, and he made a polite feint of calling Basil by some military title. He commended the trip they were about to make as the most magnificent and beautiful on the whole continent, and he commended them for intending to make it. He said that was Mrs. General Bowder of Philadelphia who just went out; did they know her? Somehow, the titles affected Basil as of older date than the late war, and as belonging to the militia period; and he imagined for the agent the romance of a life spent at a watering-place, in contact with rich money-spending, pleasure-taking people, who formed his whole jovial world. The Colonel, who included them in this world, and thereby breveted them rich and fashionable, could not secure a state-room for them on the boat,—a perfectly splendid Lake steamer, which would take them down the rapids of the St. Lawrence, and on to Montreal without change,—but he would give them a letter to the captain, who was a very *particular* friend of his, and would be happy to show them as his *friends* every attention; and so he wrote a note prescribing peculiar merits to Basil, and in spite of all reason making him feel for the moment that he was privileged by a document which was no doubt part of every such transaction. He spoke in a loud cheerful voice; he laughed jollily at no apparent joke; he bowed very low and said, "*Good*-evening!" at parting, and they went away as if he had blessed them.

The rest of the evening they spent in wandering through the village, charmed with its bizarre mixture of quaintness and commonplaces; in hanging about the shop-windows with their monotonous variety of feather fans, —each with a violently red or yellow bird painfully sacrificed in its centre,—moccasins, bead-wrought work-bags, tobacco-pouches, bows and arrows, and whatever else the savage art of the neighbouring squaws can invent; in sauntering through these gay booths, pricing many things, and in hanging long and undecidedly over cases full of feldspar crosses, quartz bracelets and necklaces, and every manner of vase, inoperative pitcher, and other vessel that can be fashioned out of the geological formation of Niagara, tormented meantime by the heat of the gas-lights and the persistence of the mosquitoes. There were very few people besides themselves in the shops, and Isabel's purchases were not lavish. Her husband had made up his mind to get her some little keepsake; and when he had taken her to the hotel he ran back to one of the shops and hastily bought her a feather fan,—a magnificent thing of deep magenta dye shading into blue, with a whole yellow-bird transfixed in the centre. When he triumphantly displayed it in their room, "Who's *that* for, Basil?" demanded his wife; "the cook?" But seeing his ghastly look at this, she fell upon his neck, crying, "O you poor old tasteless darling! You've got it for *me!*" and seemed about to die of laughter.

"Didn't you start and throw up your hands," he stammered, "when you came to that case of fans?"

"*Yes*,—in horror! Did you think I *liked* the cruel things, with their dead birds and their hideous colours? O Basil, dearest! You *are* incorrigible. *Can't* you learn that magenta is the vilest of all the hues that the perverseness of man has invented in defiance of nature? Now, my love, just promise me one thing," she said pathetically. "We're going to do a little shopping in Montreal, you know; and perhaps you'll be wanting to surprise me with something there. Don't do it. Or, if you must, do tell me all about it beforehand, and what the colour of it's to be; and I can say whether to get it or not, and then there'll be some taste about it, and I shall be *truly* surprised and pleased."

She turned to put the fan into her trunk, and he murmured something about exchanging it. "No," she said, "we'll keep it as a—a—monument." And she deposed him, with another peal of laughter, from the proud height to which he had climbed in pity of her nervous fears of the day. So completely were their places changed, that he doubted if it were not he who had made that scene on the Third Sister; and when Isabel said, "O, why *won't* men use their reasoning faculties?" he could not for himself have claimed any, and he could not urge the truth: that he had bought the fan more for its barbaric brightness than for its beauty. She would not let him get angry, and he could say nothing against the half-ironical petting with which she soothed his mortification.

But all troubles passed with the night, and the next morning they spent a charming hour about Prospect Point, and in sauntering over Goat Island, somewhat daintily tasting the flavours of the place on whose wonders they had so hungrily and indiscriminately feasted at first. They had already the feeling of veteran visitors, and they loftily marvelled at the greed with which newcomers plunged at the sensations. They could not conceive why people should want to descend the incline railway to the foot of the American Fall; they smiled at the idea of going up Terrapin Tower; they derided the vulgar daring of those who went out upon the Three Weird Sisters; for some whom they saw about to go down the Biddle Stairs to the Cave of the Winds, they had no words to express their contempt.

Then they made their excursion to the Whirlpool, mistakenly going down on the American side, for it is much better seen from the other, though seen from any point it is the most impressive feature of the whole prodigious spectacle of Niagara.

Here within the compass of a mile, those inland seas of the North, Superior, Huron, Michigan, Erie, and the multitude of smaller lakes, all pour their floods, where they swirl in dreadful vortices, with resistless undercurrents boiling beneath the surface of that mighty eddy. Abruptly from this scene of secret power, so different from the thunderous splendours of the cataract itself, rise lofty cliffs on every side, to a height of two hundred feet, clothed from the water's edge almost to their crests with dark cedars. Noiselessly, so far as your senses perceive, the lakes steal out of the whirlpool, then, drunk and wild, with brawling rapids roar away to Ontario through the narrow channel of the river. Awful as the scene is, you stand so far above it that you do not know the half of its terribleness; for those waters that look so smooth are great ridges and rings, forced, by the impulse of the currents, twelve feet higher at the centre than at the margin. Nothing can live there, and with what is caught in its hold, the maelstrom plays for days, and whirls and tosses round and round in its toils, with a sad, maniacal patience. The guides tell ghastly stories, which even their telling does not wholly rob of ghastliness, about the bodies of drowned men carried into the whirlpool and made to enact upon its dizzy surges a travesty of life, apparently floating there at their pleasure, diving and frolicking amid the waves, or frantically struggling to escape from the death that has long since befallen them.

On the American side, not far below the railway suspension bridge, is an elevator more than a hundred and eighty feet high, which is meant to let people down to the shore below, and to give a view of the rapids on their own level. From the cliff opposite, it looks a terribly frail structure of pine sticks, but is doubtless stronger than it looks; and at any rate, as it has never yet fallen to pieces, it may be pronounced perfectly safe.

In the waiting-room at the top, Basil and Isabel found Mr. Richard and his ladies again, who got into the moveable chamber with them, and they all silently descended together. It was not a time for talk of any kind, either when they were slowly and not quite smoothly dropping through the lugubrious upper part of the structure, where it was darkened by a rough weather-boarding, or lower down, where the unobstructed light showed the grim tearful face of the cliff, bedrabbled with oozy springs, and the audacious slightness of the elevator. An abiding distrust of the machinery overhead mingled in Isabel's heart with a doubt of the value of the scene below, and she could not look forward to escape from her present perils by the conveyance which had brought her into them, with any satisfaction. She wanly smiled, and shrank closer to Basil; while the other matron made nothing of seizing her husband violently by the arm and imploring him to stop it whenever they experienced a rougher jolt than usual.

At the bottom of the cliff they were helped out of their prison by a humid young Englishman, with much clay on him, whose face was red and bathed in perspiration, for it was very hot down there in his little enclosure of baking pine boards, and it was not much cooler out on the rocks upon which the party issued, descending and descending by repeated and desultory flights of steps, till at last they stood upon a huge fragment of stone right abreast of the rapids. Yet it was a magnificent sight, and for a moment none of them were sorry to have come. The surges did not look like the gigantic ripples on a river's course, as they were, but like a procession of ocean billows; they arose far aloft in vast bulks of clear green, and broke heavily into foam at the crest. Great blocks and shapeless fragments of rock strewed the margin of the awful torrent; gloomy walls of dark stone rose naked from these, bearded here and there with cedar, and everywhere frowning with shaggy brows of evergreen. The place is inexpressibly lonely and dreadful, and one feels like an alien presence there, or as if he had intruded upon some mood or haunt of Nature in which she had a right to be for ever alone. The slight, impudent structure of the elevator rises through the solitude, like a thing that merits ruin, yet it is better than something more elaborate, for it looks temporary, and since there must be an elevator, it is well to have it of the most transitory aspect. Some such quality of rude impermanence consoles you for the presence of most improvements by which you enjoy Niagara; the suspension bridges for their part being saved from offensiveness by their beauty and unreality.

Ascending, none of the party spoke; Isabel and the other matron blanched in each other's faces; their husbands maintained a stolid resignation. When they stepped out of their trap into the waiting-room at the top, "What I like about these little adventures," said Mr. Richard to Basil, abruptly, "is getting safely out of them. Good-morning, sir." He bowed slightly to Isabel, who returned his politeness, and exchanged faint nods, or glances, with the ladies. They got into their separate carriages, and at that safe distance made each other more decided obeisances.

"Well," observed Basil, "I suppose we're introduced now. We shall be meeting them from time to time throughout our journey. You know how the same faces and the same trunks used to keep turning up in our travels on the other side. Once meet people in travelling, and you can't get rid of them."

"Yes," said Isabel, as if continuing his train of thought, "I'm glad we're going to-day."

"O dearest!"

"Truly. When we first arrived I felt only the loveliness of the place. It seemed more familiar, too, then; but ever since, it's been growing stranger and dreadfuller. Somehow it's begun to pervade me and possess me in a very uncomfortable way; I'm tossed upon rapids, and flung from cataract to brinks, and dizzied in whirlpools; I'm no longer yours, Basil; I'm most unhappily married to Niagara. Fly with me, save me from my awful lord!"

She lightly burlesqued the woes of a *prima donna,* with clasped hands and uplifted eyes.

"That'll do very well," Basil commented, "and it implies a reality that can't be quite definitely spoken. We come to Niagara in the patronizing spirit in which we approach everything nowadays, and for a few hours we have it our own way, and pay our little tributes of admiration with as much complacency as we feel in acknowledging the existence of the Supreme Being. But after a while we are aware of some potent influence undermining our self-satisfaction; we begin to conjecture that the great cataract does not exist by virtue of our approval, and to feel that it will not cease when we go away. The second day makes us its abject slaves, and on the third we want to fly from it in terror. I believe some people stay for weeks, however, and hordes of them have written odes to Niagara."

"I can't understand it at all," said Isabel. "I don't wonder now that the town should be so empty this season, but that it should ever be full. I wish we'd gone after our first look at the Falls from the suspension bridge. How beautiful that was! I rejoice in everything that I haven't done. I'm so glad I haven't been in the Cave of the Winds; I'm so happy that Table Rock fell twenty years ago! Basil, I couldn't stand another rainbow to-day. I'm sorry we went out on the Three Weird Sisters. O, I shall dream about it! and the rush, and the whirl, and the dampness in one's face, and the everlasting chir-r-r-r-r of everything!"

She dipped suddenly upon his shoulder for a moment's oblivion, and then rose radiant with a question: "Why in the world, if Niagara is really what it seems to us now, do so many bridal parties come here?"

"Perhaps they're the only people who've the strength to bear up against it, and are not easily dispersed and subjected by it."

"But *we're* dispersed and subjected."

"Ah, my dear, we married a little late. Who knows how it would be if you were nineteen instead of twenty-seven, and I twenty-five and not turned of thirty?"

"Basil, you're very cruel."

"No, no. But don't you see how it is? We've known too much of life to desire any gloomy background for our happiness. We're quite contented to have things gay and bright about us. Once we couldn't have made the circle dark enough. Well, my dear, that's the effect of age. We're superannuated."

"I used to think *I* was, before we were married," answered Isabel simply; "but now," she added triumphantly, "I'm rescued from all that. I shall never be old again dearest; never, as long as you—love me!"

They were about to enter the village, and he could not

make any open acknowledgment of her tenderness; but her silken mantle (or whatever) slipped from her shoulder, and he embracingly replaced it, flattering himself that he had delicately seized this chance of an unavowed caress and not knowing (O such is the blindness of our sex!) that the opportunity had been yet more subtly afforded him, with the art which women never disuse in this world, and which I hope they will not forget in the next.

They had an early dinner, and looked their last upon the nuptial gaiety of the otherwise forlorn hotel. Three brides sat down with them in travelling-dress; two occupied the parlour as they passed out; half a dozen happy pairs arrived (to the music of the band) in the omnibus that was to carry our friends back to the station; they caught sight of several about the shop windows, as they drove through the streets. Thus the place perpetually renews itself in the glow of love as long as the summer lasts. The moon which is elsewhere so often of wormwood, or of the ordinary green cheese at the best, is of lucent honey there from the first of June to the last of October; and this is a great charm in Niagara. I think with tenderness of all the lives that have opened so fairly there; the hopes that have reigned in the glad young hearts; the measureless tide of joy that ebbs and flows with the arriving and departing trains. Elsewhere there are carking cares of business and of fashion, there are age, and sorrow, and heart-break: but here only youth, faith, rapture. I kiss my hand to Niagara for that reason, and would I were a poet for a quarter of an hour.

Isabel departed in almost a forgiving mood towards

the weak sisterhood of evident brides, and both our friends felt a lurking fondness for Niagara at the last moment. I do not know how much of their content was due to the fact that they had suffered no sort of wrong there, from those who are apt to prey upon travellers. In the hotel a placard warned them to have nothing to do with the miscreant hackmen on the streets, but always to order their carriage at the office; on the street the hackmen whispered to them not to trust the exorbitant drivers in league with the landlords; yet their actual experience was great reasonableness and facile content- ment with the sum agreed upon. This may have been because the hackmen so far outnumbered the visitors, that the latter could dictate terms; but they chose to believe it a triumph of civilization; and I will never be the cynic to sneer at their faith. Only at the station was the virtue of the Niagarans put in doubt, by the hotel porter who professed to find Basil's trunk enfeebled by travel, and advised a strap for it, which a friend of his would sell for a dollar and a half. Yet even he may have been a benevolent nature unjustly suspected.

VII.

THEY were to take the Canadian steamer at Charlotte, the port of Rochester, and they rattled uneventfully down from Niagara by rail. At the broad, low-banked river-mouth the steamer lay beside the railroad station; and while Isabel disposed of herself on board, Basil looked to the transfer of the baggage, novelly comforted in the business by the respectfulness of the young Canadian who took charge of the trunks for the boat. He was slow, and his system was not good,— he did not give checks for the pieces, but marked them with the name of their destination; and there was that indefinable something in his manner which hinted his hope that you would remember the porter; but he was so civil that he did not snub the meekest and most vexatious of the passengers, and Basil mutely blessed his servile soul. Few white Americans, he said to himself, would behave so decently in his place; and he could not conceive of the American steamboat clerk who would use the politeness towards a waiting crowd that the Canadian purser showed when they all wedged themselves in about his window to receive their state-room keys. He was somewhat awkward, like the porter, but he was patient, and he did not lose his temper even when some of the crowd, finding he would not bully them, made bold to bully him. He was three times as long in serving them

134

as an American would have been, but their time was of
no value there, and he served them well. Basil made a
point of speaking him fair, when his turn came, and the
purser did not trample on him for a base truckler, as an
American jack-in-office would have done.

Our tourists felt at home directly on this steamer,
which was very comfortable, and in every way sufficient
for its purpose, with a visible captain, who answered
two or three questions very pleasantly, and bore himself
towards his passengers in some sort like a host.

In the saloon Isabel had found among the passengers
her semi-acquaintances of the hotel parlour and the
Rapids-elevator, and had glanced tentatively towards
them. Whereupon the matron of the party had made
advances that ended in their all sitting down together,
and wondering when the boat would start, and what
time they would get to Montreal next evening, with
other matters that strangers going upon the same journey
may properly marvel over in company. The introduction having thus accomplished itself, they exchanged
addresses, and it appeared that Richard was Colonel
Ellison, of Milwaukee, and that Fanny was his wife. Miss
Kitty Ellison was of Western New York, not far from
Erie. There was a diversion presently towards the different state-rooms; but the new acquaintances sat
vis-à-vis at the table, and after supper the ladies drew
their chairs together on the promenade deck, and enjoyed the fresh evening breeze. The sun set magnificent
upon the low western shore which they had now left an
hour away, and a broad stripe of colour stretched behind
the steamer. A few thin, luminous clouds darkened mo-
mently along the horizon, and then mixed with the land.
J

The stars came out in a clear sky, and a light wind softly buffeted the cheeks, and breathed life into nerves that the day's heat had wasted. It scarcely wrinkled the tranquil expanse of the lake on which loomed, far or near, a full-sailed schooner, and presently melted into the twilight, and left the steamer solitary upon the waters. The company was small, and not remarkable enough in any way to take the thoughts of any one off his own comfort. A deep sense of the cosiness of the situation possessed them all, which was if possible intensified by the spectacle of the captain, seated on the upper deck, and smoking a cigar that flashed and fainted like a stationary fire-fly in the gathering dusk. How very distant, in this mood, were the most recent events! Niagara seemed a fable of antiquity; the ride from Rochester a myth of the Middle Ages. In this cool, happy world of quiet lake, of starry skies, of air that the soul itself seemed to breathe, there was such consciousness of repose as if one were steeped in rest and soaked through and through with calm.

The points of likeness between Isabel and Mrs. Ellison shortly made them mutually uninteresting, and, leaving her husband to the others, Isabel frankly sought the companionship of Miss Kitty, in whom she found a charm of manner which puzzled at first, but which she presently fancied must be perfect trust of others mingling with a peculiar self-reliance.

"Can't you see, Basil what a very flattering way it is?" she asked of her husband, when, after parting with their friends for the night, she tried to explain the character to him. "Of course no art could equal such a natural gift; for that kind of belief in your good-nature and sympathy makes you feel worthy of it, don't you know; and so you can't help being good-natured and sympathetic. This Miss Ellison, why, I can tell you, I shouldn't be ashamed of her anywhere." By anywhere Isabel meant Boston, and she went on to praise the young lady's intelligence and refinement, with those expressions of surprise at the existence of civilisation in a westerner which westerners find it so hard to receive graciously. Happily, Miss Ellison had not to hear them. "The reason she happened to come with only two dresses is, she lives so near Niagara that she could come for one day, and go back the next. The colonel's her cousin, and he and his wife go East every year, and they asked her this time to see Niagara with them. She told me all over again what we eavesdropped so shamefully in the hotel parlour; and I don't know whether she was better pleased with the prospect of what's before her, or with the notion of making the journey in this original way. She didn't force her confidence upon me, any more than she tried to withhold it. We got to talking in the most natural manner; and she seemed to tell these things about herself because they amused her and she liked me. I had been saying how my trunk got left behind once on the French side of Mont Cenis, and I had to wear aunt's things at Turin till it could be sent for."

"Well, I don't see but Miss Ellison could describe you to her friends very much as you've described her to me," said Basil. "How did these mutual confidences begin? Whose trustfulness first flattered the other's? What else did you tell about yourself?"

"I said we were on our wedding journey," guiltily admitted Isabel.

"O, you did!"

"Why, dearest! I wanted to know, for once, you see, whether we seemed honeymoon-struck."

"And do we?"

"No," came the answer, somewhat ruefully. "Perhaps, Basil," she added, "we've been a little *too* successful in disguising our bridal character. Do you know," she continued, looking him anxiously in the face, "this Miss Ellison took me at first for—your sister.

Basil broke forth in outrageous laughter. "One more such victory," he said, "and we are undone;" and he laughed again immoderately. "How sad is the fruition of human wishes! There's nothing, after all, like a good thorough failure for making people happy."

Isabel did not listen to him. Safe in a dim corner of the deserted saloon, she seized him in a vindictive embrace; then, as if it had been he who suggested the idea of such a loathsome relation, hissed out the hated words, "Your sister!" and released him with a disdainful repulse.

A little after daybreak the steamer stopped at the Canadian city of Kingston, a handsome place, substantial to the water's edge, and giving a sense of English solidity by the stone of which it is largely built. There was an accession of many passengers here, and they and the people on the wharf were as little like Americans as possible. They were English or Irish or Scotch, with the healthful bloom of the Old World still upon their faces, or if Canadians they looked not less hearty; so that one must wonder if the line between the Dominion and the United States did not sharply separate good digestion and dyspepsia. These provincials had not our regularity of features, nor the best of them our careworn sensibility of expression; but neither had they our complexions of *adobe;* and even Isabel was forced to allow that the men were, on the whole, better dressed than the same number of average Americans would have been in a city of that size and remoteness. The stevedores who were putting the freight aboard were men of leisure; they joked in a kindly way with the orange-woman and the old woman picking up chips on the pier; and our land of hurry seemed beyond the ocean rather than beyond the lake.

Kingston has romantic memories of being Fort Frontenac two hundred years ago; of Count Frontenac's splendid advent among the Indians; of the brave La Salle, who turned its wooden walls to stone; of wars with the savages and then with the New York colonists, whom the French and their allies harried from this point; of the destruction of La Salle's fort in the Old French War; and of final surrender a few years later to the English. It is as picturesque as it is historical. All about the city the shores are beautifully wooded, and there are many lovely islands,—the first indeed of those Thousand Islands with which the head of the St. Lawrence is filled, and among which the steamer was presently threading her way. They are still as charming and still almost as wild as when, in 1673, Frontenac's flotilla of canoes passed through their labyrinth and issued upon the lake. Save for a light-house upon one of them, there is almost nothing to show that the foot of man has ever pressed the thin grass clinging to their rocky surfaces, and keeping its green in the eternal shadow of their pines and cedars. In the warm morning light they gathered or dispersed before the advancing vessel which some of

them almost touched with the plumage of their evergreens; and where none of them were large, some were
so small that it would not have been too bold to figure
them as a vaster race of water-birds assembling and
separating in her course. It is curiously affecting to find
them so unclaimed yet from the solitude of the vanished
wilderness, and scarcely touched even by tradition. But
for the interest left them by the French, these tiny
islands have scarcely any associations, and must be enjoyed for their beauty alone. There is indeed about
them a faint light of legend concerning the Canadian
rebellion of 1837, for several patriots are said to have
taken refuge amidst their lovely multitude; but this
episode of modern history is difficult for the imagination
to manage, and somehow one does not take sentimentally
even to that daughter of a lurking patriot, who long
baffled her father's pursuers by rowing him from one
island to another, and supplying him with food by night.

Either the reluctance is from the natural desire that
so recent a heroine should be founded on fact, or it is
mere perverseness. Perhaps I ought to say, in justice to
her, that it was one of her own sex who refused to be interested in her, and forbade Basil to care for her. When
he had read of her exploit from the guide-book, Isabel
asked him if he had noticed that handsome girl in the
blue and white striped Garibaldi and Swiss hat, who
had come aboard at Kingston. She pointed her out, and
courageously made him admire her beauty, which was
of the most bewitching Canadian type. The young girl
was redeemed by her New World birth from the English
heaviness; a more delicate bloom lighted her cheeks;
a softer grace dwelt in her movements; yet

she was round and full, and she was in the perfect
flower of youth. She was not so ethereal in her loveliness
as an American girl, but she was not so nervous, and
had none of the painful fragility of the latter. Her expression was just a little vacant, it must be owned; but
so far as she went she was faultless. She looked like
the most tractable of daughters, and as if she would be
the most obedient of wives. She had a blameless taste
in dress, Isabel declared; her costume of blue and white
striped Garibaldi and Swiss hat (set upon heavy masses
of dark brown hair) being completed by a black silk
skirt. "And you can see," she added, "that it's an old
skirt made over, and that she's dressed as cheaply
as she is prettily." This surprised Basil, who
had imputed the young lady's personal sumptu-
ousness to her dress, and had thought it enormously rich. When she got off with her *chaperon*
at one of the poorest-looking country landings, she
left them in hopeless conjecture about her. Was she
visiting there, or was the interior of Canada full of such
stylish and exquisite creatures? Where did she get her
taste, her fashions, her manners? As she passed from
sight towards the shadow of the woods, they felt the
poorer for her going; yet they were glad to have seen
her, and on second thoughts they felt that they could
not justly ask more of her than to have merely existed
for a few hours in their presence. They perceived that
beauty was not only its own excuse for being, but that
it flattered and favoured and profited the world by con-
senting to be.

At Prescott, the boat on which they had come from
Charlotte, and on which they had been promised a pas-

sage without change to Montreal, stopped, and they were transferred to a smaller steamer with the uncomfortable name of Banshee. She was very old, and very infirm and dirty, and in every way bore out the character of a squalid Irish goblin. Besides, she was already heavily laden with passengers, and, with the addition of the other steamer's people had now double her complement; and our friends doubted if they were not to pass the Rapids in as much danger as discomfort. Their fellow-passengers were in great variety, however, and thus partly atoned for their numbers. Among them of course there was a full force of brides from Niagara and elsewhere, and some curious forms of the prevailing infatuation appeared. It is well enough, if she likes, and it may be very noble for a passably good-looking young lady to marry a gentleman of venerable age; but to intensify the idea of self-devotion by furtively caressing his wrinkled front seems too reproachful of the general public; while, on the other hand, if the bride is very young and pretty, it enlists in behalf of the white-haired husband the unwilling sympathies of the spectator to see her the centre of a group of young people, and him only acknowledged from time to time by a Parthian snub. Nothing, however, could have been more satisfactory than the sisterly surrounding of this latter bride. They were of a better class of Irish people; and if it had been any sacrifice for her to marry so old a man, they were doing their best to give the affair at least the liveliness of a wake. There were five or six of those great handsome girls, with their generous curves and wholesome colours, and they were every one attended by a good-looking colonial lover, with whom they joked in slightly brogued voices, and laughed with careless Celtic laughter. One of the young fellows presently lost his hat overboard, and had to wear the handkerchief of his lady about his head; and this appeared to be really one of the best things in the world, and led to endless banter. They were well dressed, and it could be imagined that the ancient bridegroom had come in for the support of the whole good-looking, healthy, light-hearted family. In some degree he looked it, and wore but a rueful countenance for a bridegroom; so that a very young newly married couple, who sat next the jolly sister-and-loverhood, could not keep their pitying eyes off his downcast face. "What if he, too, were young at heart!" the kind little wife's regard seemed to say.

For the sake of the slight air that was stirring, and to have the best view of the Rapids, the Banshee's whole company was gathered upon the forward promenade, and the throng was almost as dense as in a six-o'clock horse-car out from Boston. The standing and sitting groups were closely packed together, and the expanded parasols and umbrellas formed a nearly unbroken roof. Under this Isabel chatted at intervals with the Ellisons, who sat near; but it was not an atmosphere that provoked social feeling, and she was secretly glad when after a while they shifted their position.

It was deadly hot, and most of the people saddened and silenced in the heat. From time to time the clouds idling about overhead met and sprinkled down a cruel little shower of rain that seemed to make the air less breathable than before. The lonely shores were yellow with drought; the islands grew wilder and barrener; the course of the river was for miles at a stretch through

country which gave no signs of human life. The St.
Lawrence has none of the bold picturesqueness of the
Hudson, and is far more like its far-off cousin the
Mississippi. Its banks are low like the Mississippi's, its current swift, its way through solitary
lands. The same sentiment of early adventure hangs
about each : both are haunted by visions of the Jesuit in
his priestly robe, and the soldier in his mediæval steel ;
the same gay, devout, and dauntless race has touched
them both with immortal romance. If the water were of
a dusky golden colour, instead of translucent green, and
the shores and islands were covered with cottonwoods
and willows instead of dark cedars, one could with no
great effort believe one's self on the Mississippi between
Cairo and St. Louis, so much do the great rivers strike
one as kindred in the chief features of their landscape.
Only, in tracing this resemblance you do not know just
what to do with the purple mountains of Vermont, seen
vague against the horizon from the St. Lawrence, or
with the quaint little French villages that begin to show
themselves as you penetrate further down into Lower
Canada. These look so peaceful, with their dormer-
windowed cottages clustering about their church-spires,
that it seems impossible they could once have been the
homes of the savages and the cruel peasants who, with
fire-brand and scalping-knife and tomahawk, harassed
the borders of New England for a hundred years. But
just after you descend the Long Sault you pass the
hamlet of St. Regis, in which was kindled the torch that
wrapt Deerfield in flames, waking her people from their
sleep to meet instant death or taste the bitterness of a
captivity. The bell which was sent out from France for

the Indian converts of the Jesuits, and was captured
by an English ship and carried into Salem, and thence
sold to Deerfield, where it called the Puritans to prayer,
till at last it also summoned the priest-led Indians and
habitans across hundreds of miles of winter and of
wilderness to reclaim it from that desecration,—this fateful bell still hangs in the church-tower of St. Regis, and
has invited to matins and vespers for nearly two
centuries the children of those who fought so pitilessly
and dared and endured so much for it.   Our friends
would fain have heard it as they passed, hoping for
some mournful note of history in its sound; but it hung
silent over the silent hamlet, which, as it lay in the hot
afternoon sun by the river's side, seemed as lifeless as the
Deerfield burnt long ago.

They turned from it to look at a gentleman who had
appeared in a mustard-coloured linen duster, and Basil
asked, "Shouldn't you like to know the origin, personal
history, and secret feelings of a gentleman who goes
about in a duster of that particular tint? Or, that gentleman yonder with his eye tied up in a wet handkerchief,
do you suppose he's travelling for pleasure? Look at
those young people from Omaha: they haven't ceased
flirting or cackling since we left Kingston. Do you think
everybody has such spirits out at Omaha? But behold a
yet more surprising figure than any we have yet seen
among this boat-load of nondescripts!"

This was a tall, handsome young man, with a face of
somewhat foreign cast, and well dressed, with a certain
impressive difference from the rest in the cut of his
clothes.   But what most drew the eye to him was a large
cross, set with brilliants, and surmounted by a heavy

double-headed eagle in gold. This ornament dazzled from a conspicuous place on the left lappel of his coat; on his hand shone a magnificent diamond ring, and he bore a stately opera-glass, with which, from time to time, he imperiously, as one may say, surveyed the landscape. As the imposing apparition grew upon Isabel, "O here," she thought, ,"is something truly distinguished. Of course, dear," she added aloud to Basil, "he's some foreign nobleman travelling here;" and she ran over in her mind the newspaper announcements of patrician visitors from abroad, and tried to identify him with some of them. The cross must be the decoration of a foreign order, and Basil suggested that he was perhaps a member of some legation at Washington, who had run up there for his summer vacation. The cross puzzled him, but the double-headed eagle, he said, meant either Austria or Russia; probably Austria, for the wearer looked a trifle too civilized for a Russian.

"Yes, indeed! What an air he *has!* Never tell *me*, Basil, that there's nothing in *blood!*" cried Isabel, who was a bitter aristocrat at heart, like all her sex, though in principle she was democratic enough. As she spoke, the object of her regard looked about him on the different groups, not with pride not with hauteur, but with a glance of unconscious, unmistakable superiority. "O, that stare!" she added; "nothing but high birth and long descent can give it! Dearest, he's becoming a great affliction to me. I want to know who he is. Couldn't you invent some pretext for speaking to him?"

"No, I couldn't do it decently; and no doubt he'd snub me as I deserved if I intruded upon him. Let's wait for fortune to reveal him."

"Well, I suppose I must, but it's dreadful; it's really

dreadful. You can easily see *that's* distinction," she continued, as her hero moved about the promenade and gently but loftily made a way for himself among the other passengers and favoured the scenery through his opera-glass from one point and another. He spoke to no one and she reasonably supposed that he did not know English.

In the meantime it was drawing near the hour of dinner, but no dinner appeared. Twelve, one, two came and went, and then at last came the dinner, which had been delayed it seemed, till the cook could recruit his energies sufficiently to meet the wants of double the number he had expected to provide for. It was observable of the officers and crew of the Banshee, that while they did not hold themselves aloof from the passengers in the disdainful American manner, they were of feeble mind, and not only did everything very slowly (in the usual Canadian fashion), but with an inefficiency that among us would have justified them in being insolent. The people sat down at several successive tables to the worst dinner that ever was cooked; the ladies first and the gentlemen afterwards, as they made conquest of places. At the second table, to Basil's great satisfaction, he found a seat, and on his right hand the distinguished foreigner.

"Naturally, I was somewhat abashed," he said in the account he was presently called to give Isabel of the interview, "but I remembered that I was an American citizen, and tried to maintain a decent composure. For several minutes we sat silent behind a dish of flabby cucumbers, expecting the dinner, and I was wondering whether I should address him in French or German,—

for I knew you'd never forgive me if I let slip such a
chance,—when he turned and spoke himself."

"Oh, *what* did he say, dearest?"

"He said, 'Pretty tedious waitin', ain't it?' in the best
New York State accent."

"You don't mean it!" gasped Isabel.

"But I do. After that I took courage to ask what his
cross and double-headed eagle meant. He showed the
condescension of a true nobleman. 'O,' says he, 'I'm glad
you like it, and it's not the least offence to ask,' and he
told me. Can you imagine what it is? It's the emblem
of the fifty-fourth degree in the secret society he belongs
to!"

"I don't believe it!"

"Well, ask him yourself, then,' returned Basil; "he's
a very good fellow. 'O, that stare; nothing but high
birth and long descent could give it;'" he repeated,
abominably implying that he had himself had no share
in their common error.

What retort Isabel might have made cannot now be
known, for she was arrested at this moment by a rumour
amongst the passengers that they were coming to the
Long Sault Rapids. Looking forward she saw the tossing
and flashing of surges that, to the eye, are certainly as
threatening as the rapids above Niagara. The steamer
had already passed the Deplau and the Galopes, and
they had thus had a foretaste of whatever pleasure or
terror there is in the descent of these nine miles of
stormy sea. It is purely a matter of taste, about shoot-
ing the rapids of the St. Lawrence. The passengers like
it better than the captain and the pilot, to guess by their
looks, and the women and children like it better than the

men. It is no doubt very thrilling and picturesque and
wildly beautiful; the children crow and laugh, the women shout forth their delight as the boat enters the seeth-
ing current; great foaming waves strike her bows, and
brawl away to the stern, while she dips and rolls, and
shoots onward, light as a bird blown by the wind; the
wild shores and islands whirl out of sight; you feel in
every fibre the career of the vessel. But the captain sits
in front of the pilot-house smoking with a grave face,
the pilots tug hard at the wheel; the hoarse roar of the
waters fills the air; beneath the smoother sweeps of the
current you can see the brown rocks; as you sink from
ledge to ledge in the writhing and twisting steamer, you
have a vague sense that all this is perhaps an achieve-
ment rather than an enjoyment. When, descending the
Long Sault, you look back up-hill, and behold those billows leaping down the steep slope after you, "No doubt,"
you confide to your soul, "it is magnificent; but it is not
pleasure." You greet with silent satisfaction the level
river, stretching between the Long Sault and the Coteau,
and you admire the delightful tranquillity of that beautiful Lake St. Francis into which it expands. Then the
boat shudders into the Coteau Rapids, and down through
the Cedars and Cascades. On the rocks of the last lies
the skeleton of a steamer wrecked upon them, and
gnawed at still by the white-tusked wolfish rapids. No
one, they say, was lost from her. "But how," Basil
thought' "would it fare with all these people packed here
upon her bow, if the Banshee should swing round upon
a ledge?" As to Isabel, she looked upon the wrecked
steamer with indifference, as did all the women; but
then they could not swim, and would not have to save

themselves. "The La Chine's to come yet," they exulted, "and that's the awfullest of all!"

They passed the Lake St. Louis; the La Chine Rapids flashed into sight. The captain rose up from his seat, took his pipe from his mouth, and waved a silence with it. "Ladies and gentlemen," said he, "it's very important in passing these rapids to keep the boat perfectly trim. Please to remain just as you are."

It was twilight, for the boat was late. From the Indian village on the shore they signalled to know if he wanted the local pilot; the captain refused; and then the steamer plunged into the leaping waves. From rock to rock she swerved and sank; on the last ledge she scraped with a deadly touch that went to the heart.

Then the danger was past, and the noble city of Montreal was in full sight, lying at the foot of her dark green mountain, and lifting her many spires into the rosy twilight air; massive and grand showed the sister towers of the French cathedral.

Basil had hoped to approach this famous city with just associations. He had meant to conjure up for Isabel's sake some reflex, however faint, of that beautiful picture Mr. Parkman has painted of Maisonneuve founding and consecrating Montreal. He flushed with the recollection of the historian's phrase; but in that moment there came forth from the cabin a pretty young person who gave every token of being a pretty young actress, even to the duenna-like, elderly female companion, to be detected in the remote background of every young actress. She had flirted audaciously during the day with some young Englishmen and Canadians of her acquaintance, and after passing the La Chine Rapids she had taken the hearts of all the men by springing suddenly to her feet, apostrophising the tumult with a charming attitude, and warbling a delicious bit of song. Now as they drew near the city the Victoria Bridge stretched its long tube athwart the river, and looked so low because of its great length that it seemed to bar the steamer's passage.

"I wonder," said one of the actress's adorers,—a Canadian, whose face was exactly that of the beaver on the the escutcheon of his native province, and whose heavy gallantries she had constantly received with a gay, impertinent nonchalance,—"I wonder if we can be going right under that bridge?"

"No, sir!" answered the pretty young actress with shocking promptness, "we're going right over it:—

> " 'Three groans and a guggle,
> And an awful struggle,
> And over we go!' "

At this witless, sweet impudence the Canadian looked very sheepish—for a beaver; and all the other people laughed; but the noble historical shades of Basil's thoughts vanished in wounded dignity beyond recall, and left him feeling rather ashamed,—for he had laughed, too.

K

VIII.

THE feeling of foreign travel for which our tourists had striven throughout their journey, and which they had known in some degree at Kingston and all the way down the river, was intensified from the first moment in Montreal; and it was so welcome that they were almost glad to lose money on their greenbacks, which the conductor of the omnibus would take only at a discount of twenty cents. At breakfast next morning they could hardly tell on what country they had fallen. The waiters had but a thin varnish of English speech upon their native French, and they spoke their own tongue with each other; but most of the meats were cooked to the English taste, and the whole was a poor imitation of an American hotel. During their stay the same commingling of usages and races bewildered them; the shops were English and the clerks were commonly French; the carriage-drivers were often Irish, and up and down the streets with their pious old-fashioned names tinkled American horsecars. Everywhere were churches and convents that recalled the ecclesiastical and feudal origin of the city; the great tubular bridge, the superb water-front with its long array of docks only surpassed by those of Liverpool, the solid blocks of business houses, and the substantial mansions on the quieter streets, proclaimed the succession of Protestant thrift and energy.

Our friends cared far less for the modern splendour of Montreal than for the remnants of its past, and for the features that identified it with another faith and another people than their own. Isabel would almost have confessed to any one of the black-robed priests upon the street; Basil could easily have gone down upon his knees to the white-hooded, pale-faced nuns gliding among the crowd. It was rapture to take a carriage, and drive, not to the cemetery, not to the public library, not to the rooms of the Young Men's Christian Association, or the grain elevators, or the new park just tricked out with rockwood and sprigs of evergreen,—not to any of the charming resorts of our own cities, but as in Europe to the churches, the churches of a pitiless superstition, the churches with their atrocious pictures and statues, their lingering smell of the morning's incense, their confessionals, their fee-taking sacristans, their worshippers dropped here and there upon their knees about the aisles and saying their prayers with shut or wandering eyes according as they were old women or young! I do not defend the feeble sentimentality,—call it wickedness if you like,—but I understand it and I forgive it from my soul.

They went first, of course, to the French cathedral, pausing on their way to alight and walk through the Bonsecours Market, where the *habitans* have all come in their carts, with their various stores of poultry, fruit, and vegetables, and where every cart is a study. Here is a simple-faced young peasant-couple with butter and eggs and chickens ravishingly displayed; here is a smooth-cheeked, black-eyed, black-haired young girl, looking as if an infusion of Indian blood had darkened the red of her cheeks, presiding over a stock of onions, potatoes, beets, and turnips; there an old woman with a face carven like a walnut, behind a flattering array of cherries and pears; yonder a whole family trafficking in loaves of brown-bread and maple-sugar in many shapes of pious and grotesque device. There are gay shows of bright scarfs and kerchiefs and vari-coloured yarns, and sad shows of old clothes and second-hand merchandise of other sorts; but above all prevails the abundance of orchard and garden, while within the fine edifice are the stalls of the butchers, and in the basement below a world of household utensils, glass-ware, hardware, and wooden ware. As in other Latin countries, each peasant has given a personal interest to his wares, but the bargains are not clamoured over as in Latin lands abroad. Whatever protest and concession and invocation of the saints attend the transaction of business at Bonsecours Market are in a subdued tone. The fat huckster-women drowsing beside their wares, scarce send their voices beyond the borders of their broad-brimmed straw hats, as they softly haggle with purchasers, or tranquilly gossip together.

At the cathedral there are, perhaps, the worst paintings in the world and the massive pine-board pillars are unscrupulously smoked to look like marble; but our tourists enjoyed it as if it had been St. Peter's; in fact it has something of the barn-like immensity and impressiveness of St. Peter's. They did not ask it to be beautiful or grand; they desired it only to recall the beloved ugliness, the fondly cherished hideousness and incongruity

of the average Catholic churches of their remembrance,
and it did this and more; it added an effect of its own;
it offered the spectacle of a swarthy old Indian kneeling
before the high altar, telling his beads, and saying with
many sighs and tears the prayers which it cost so much
martyrdom and heroism to teach his race. "O, it is only
a savage man," said the little French boy who was showing them the place, impatient of their interest in a thing
so unworthy as this groaning barbarian. He ran swiftly
about from object to object, rapidly lecturing their in-
attention. "It is now time to go up into the tower," said
he, and they gladly made that toilsome ascent, though it
is doubtful if the ascent of towers is not too much
like the ascent of mountains ever to be compensatory.
From the top of Notre Dame is certainly to
be had a prospect upon which, but for his fluttered
nerves and trembling muscles and troubled respiration,
the traveller might well look with delight, and as it is
must behold with wonder. So far as the eye reaches it
dwells only upon what is magnificent. All the features
of that landscape are grand. Below you spreads the city,
which has less that is merely mean in it than any other
city of our continent, and which is everywhere ennobled
by stately civic edifices, adorned by tasteful churches,
and skirted by full-foliaged avenues of mansions and
villas. Behind it rises the beautiful mountain, green
with woods and gardens to its crest, and flanked on the
east by an endless fertile plain, and on the west by another expanse, through which the Ottawa rushes, turbid
and dark, to its confluence with the St. Lawrence. Then
these two mighty streams commingled flow past the city,
lighting up the vast champaign country to the south,

while upon the utmost southern verge, as on the northern, rise the cloudy summits of far-off mountains.

As our travellers gazed upon all this grandeur, their hearts were humbled to the tacit admission that the colonial metropolis was not only worthy of its seat, but had traits of a solid prosperity not excelled by any of the abounding and boastful cities of the Republic. Long before they quitted Montreal they had rallied from this weakness, but they delighted still to honour her superb beauty.

The tower is naturally bescribbled to its top with the names of those who have climbed it, and most of these are Americans, who flock in great numbers to Canada in summer. They modify its hotel life, and the objects of interest thrive upon their bounty. Our friends met them at every turn, and knew them at a glance from the native populations, who are also easily distinguishable from each other. The French Canadians are nearly always of a peasant-like commonness, or where they rise above this have a burgeois commonness of face and manner; and the English Canadians are to be known from the many English sojourners by the effort to look much more English than the latter. The social heart of the colony clings fast to the mother-country, that is plain, whatever the political tendency may be; and the public monuments and inscriptions celebrate this affectionate union.

At the English cathedral the effect is deepened by the epitaphs of those whose lives were passed in the joint service of England and her loyal child; and our travellers, whatever their want of sympathy with the sentiment, had to own to a certain beauty in that attitude of proud reverence. Here, at least, was a people not cut off from its past, but holding, unbroken in life and death, the ties which exist for us only in history. It gave a glamour of olden time to the new land; it touched the prosaic democratic present with the warning poetic light of the aristocratic and monarchial tradition. There was here and there a title on the tablets, and there was everywhere the formal language of loyalty and of veneration for things we have tumbled into the dust. It is a beautiful church, of admirable English Gothic; if you are so happy, you are rather curtly told you may enter by a burly English figure in some kind of sombre ecclesiastical drapery, and within its quiet precincts you may feel yourself in England if you like,—which, for my part, I do not. Neither did our friends enjoy it so much as the Church of the Jesuits, with its more than tolerable paintings, its coldly frescoed ceiling, its architectural taste of subdued Renaissance, and its black-eyed peasant-girl telling her beads before a side altar, just as in the enviably deplorable countries we all love; nor so much even as the Irish cathedral which they next visited. That is a very gorgeous cathedral indeed, painted and gilded *a merveille,* and everywhere stuck about with big and little saints and crucifixes, and pictures incredibly bad—but for those in the French cathedral. There is, of course, a series representing Christ's progress to Calvary; and there was a very tattered old man,—an old man whose voice had been long ago drowned in whiskey, and who now spoke in a ghostly whisper,—who, when he saw Basil's eye fall upon the series, made him go the round of them, and tediously explained them.

"Why did you let that old wretch bore you, and then pay him for it?" Isabel asked.

"O, it reminded me so sweetly of the swindles of other lands and days, that I couldn't help it," he answered; and straightway in the eyes of both that poor, whiskey-fied, Irish tatterdemalion stood transfigured to the glorious likeness of an Italian beggar.

They were always doing something of this kind, those absurdely sentimental people, whom yet I cannot find it in my heart to blame for their folly, though I could name ever so many reasons for rebuking it. Why, in fact, should we wish to find America like Europe? Are the ruins and impostures and miseries and superstitions which beset the traveller abroad so precious that he should desire to imagine them at every step in his own hemisphere? Or have we then of our own no effective shapes of ignorance and want and incredibility, that we must for ever seek an alien contrast to our native intelligence and comfort? Some such questions this guilty couple put to each other, and then drove off to visit the convent of the Grey Nuns with a joyful expectation which I suppose the prospect of the finest public school exhibition in Boston could never have inspired. But, indeed, since there must be Grey Nuns, is it not well that there are sentimentalists to take a mournful pleasure in their sad, pallid existence?

The convent is at a good distance from the Irish cathedral, and in going to it the tourists made their driver carry them through one of the few old French streets which still remain in Montreal. Fires and improvements had made havoc among the quaint houses since Basil's first visit; but at last they came upon a narrow, ancient Rue Saint Antoine,—or whatever other saint it was called after,—in which there was no English face or house to be seen. The doors of the little one-story dwellings opened from the pavement, and within you saw fat madame the mother moving about her domestic affairs, and spare monsieur the elderly husband smoking beside the open window; French babies crawled about the tidy floors; French martyrs (let us believe Lalement or Brébeuf, who gave up their heroic lives for the conversion of Canada) lifted their eyes in high-coloured lithographs on the wall; among the flowerpots in the dormer-window looking from every tin roof sat and sewed a smooth-haired young girl, I hope,—the romance of each little mansion. The antique and foreign character of the place was accented by the inscription upon a wall of "Sirop adoucissant de Madame Winslow."

Ever since 1692 the Grey Nuns have made a refuge within the ample borders of their convent for infirm old people and for foundling children, and it is now in the regular course of sight-seeing for the traveller to visit their hospital at noonday, when he beholds the Sisters at their devotions in the chapel. It is a bare, white-walled, cold-looking chapel, with the usual paraphernalia of pictures and crucifixes. Seated upon low benches on either side of the aisle were the curious or the devout; the former in greater number and chiefly Americans, who were now and then whispered silent by an old pauper zealous for the sanctity of the place. At the stroke of twelve the Sisters entered two by two, followed by the lady-superior with a prayer-book in her hand. She clapped the leaves of this together in signal for them to kneel, to rise, to kneel again and rise, while they repeated in rather harsh voices their prayers, and then clattered out of the chapel as they had clattered in, with resounding shoes. The two young girls at the head were very pretty, and all the pale faces had a corpse-like peace. As Basil looked at their pensive sameness, it seemed to him that those prettiest girls might very well be the twain that he had seen there so many years ago, stricken for ever young in their joyless beauty. The ungraceful gowns of coarse grey, the blue checkered aprons, the black crape caps, were the same; they came and went with the same quick tread, touching their brows with holy water and kneeling and rising now as then with the same constrained and ordered movements. Would it be too cruel if they were really the same persons? or would it be yet more cruel if every year two girls so young and fair were self-doomed to renew the likeness of that youthful death?

The visitors went about the hospital, and saw the old men and the little children to whom these good pure lives were given, and they could only blame the system, not the instruments or their work. Perhaps they did not judge wisely of the amount of self-sacrifice involved, for they judged from hearts to which love was the whole of earth and heaven; but nevertheless they pitied the Grey Nuns amidst the unhomelike comfort of their convent, the unnatural care of those alien little ones. Poor Sœurs Grises! in their narrow cells; at the bedside of sickness and age and sorrow; kneeling with clasped hands and yearning eyes before the bloody spectacle of the cross!—the power of your Church is shown far more subtly and mightily in such as you, than in her grandest fanes or the sight of her most august ceremonies, with praying priests, swinging censers, tapers and pictures and images, under a gloomy heaven of cathedral arches. There, indeed, the faithful have given their substance; but here the nun has given up the most precious part of her woman's nature, and all the tenderness that clings about the thought of wife and mother.

"There are some things that always greatly afflict me in the idea of a new country," said Basil, as they loitered slowly through the grounds of the convent toward the gate. "Of course, it's absurd to think of men as other than men, as having changed their natures with their skies; but a new land always does seem at first thoughts like a new chance afforded the race for goodness and happiness, for health and life. So I grieve for the earliest dead at Plymouth more than for the multitude that the plague swept away in London; I shudder over the crime of the first guilty man, the sin of the first wicked woman in a new country; the trouble of the first youth or maiden crossed in love there is intolerable. All should be hope and freedom and prosperous life upon that virgin soil. It never was so since Eden; but none the less I feel it ought to be; and I am oppressed by the thought that among the earliest walls which rose upon this broad meadow of Montreal were those built to immure the innocence of such young girls as these, and shut them from the life we find so fair. Wouldn't you like to know who was the first that took the veil in this wild new country? Who was she, poor soul, and what was her deep sorrow or lofty rapture? You can fancy her some Indian maiden lured to the renunciation by the splendour of symbols and promises seen vaguely through the lingering mists of her native superstitions; or some weary soul, sick from the vanities and vices, the bloodshed and the tears of the Old World, and eager for a silence profounder than that of the wilderness into which she had fled. Well, the Church knows and God. She was dust long ago."

From time to time there had fallen little fitful showers during the morning. Now as the wedding-journeyers passed out of the convent gate the rain dropped soft and thin, and the grey clouds, that floated through the sky so swiftly were as far-seen Grey Sisters in flight for heaven.

"We shall have time for the drive round the mountain before dinner," said Basil, as they got into their carriage again; and he was giving the order to the driver, when Isabel asked how far it was.

"Nine miles."

"O, then we can't think of going with one horse. You know," she added, "that we always intended to have two horses for going round the mountain."

"No," said Basil, not yet used to having his decisions reached without his knowledge. "And I don't see why we should. Everybody goes with one. You don't suppose we're too heavy, do you?"

"I had a party from the States, ma'am, yesterday," interposed the driver; "two ladies, real heavy ones, two gentlemen, weighin' two hundred apiece, and a stout young man on the box with me. You'd 'a' thought the horse was drawin' an empty carriage, the way she darted along."

"Then his horse must be perfectly worn out to-day," said Isabel, refusing to admit the poor fellow directly even to the honours of a defeat. He had proved too

much, and was put out of court with no hope of repair-
ing his error.

"Why, it seems a pity," whispered Basil dispassionate-
ly, "to turn this man adrift, when he had a reasonable
hope of being with us all day, and has been so civil and
obliging."

"O yes, Basil, sentimentalize him, do! Why don't you
sentimentalize his helpless, overworked horse?—all in a
reek of perspiration."

"Perspiration! Why, my dear, it's the rain!"

"Well, rain or shine, darling, I don't want to go round
the mountain with one horse; and it's very unkind of
you to insist now, when you've tacitly promised me all
along to take two."

"Now, this is a little too much, Isabel. You know we
never mentioned the matter till this moment."

"It's the same as a promise, your not saying you
wouldn't. But I don't *ask* you to keep your word. *I*
don't want to go round the mountain. I'd *much* rather
go to the hotel. I'm tired.

"Very well, then, Isabel, I'll leave you at the hotel."

In a moment it had come, the first serious dispute of
their wedded life. It had come as all such calamities
come, from nothing, and it was on them in full disaster
ere they knew. Such a very little while ago, there in the
convent garden, their lives had been drawn closer in
sympathy than ever before; and now that blessed time
seemed ages since, and they were further asunder than
those who have never been friends. "I thought," bit-
terly mused Isabel, "that he would have done anything
for me." "Who could have dreamed that a woman of
her sense would be so unreasonable?" he wondered. Both

had tempers, as I know my dearest reader has (if a lady),
and neither would yield; and so, presently, they could
hardly tell how, for they were aghast at it all, Isabel was
alone in her room amidst the ruins of her life, and Basil
alone in the one-horse carriage, trying to drive away
from the wreck of his happiness. All was over; the
dream was past; the charm was broken. The sweetness
of their love was turned to gall; whatever had pleased
them in their loving moods was loathsome now, and the
things they had praised a moment before were hateful.
In that baleful light, which seemed to dwell upon all
they ever said or did in mutual enjoyment, how poor and
stupid and empty looked their wedding-journey! Basil
spent five minutes in arraigning his wife and convicting
her of every folly and fault. His soul was in a whirl,—

> "For to be wroth with one we love
> Doth work like madness in the brain.'

In the midst of his bitter and furious upbraidings he
found himself suddenly become her ardent advocate, and
ready to denounce her judge as a heartless monster.
"On our wedding journey, too! Good heavens, what an
incredible brute I am!" Then he said, "What an ass I
am!" And the pathos of the case having yielded to its
absurdity, he was helpless. In five minutes more he was
at Isabel's side, the one-horse carriage driver dismissed
with a handsome *pour-boire,* and a pair of lusty bays
with a glittering barouche waiting at the door below. He
swiftly accounted for his presence, which she seemed to
find the most natural thing that could be, and she met
his surrender with the openness of a heart that forgives
but does not forget, if indeed the most gracious art is
the only one unknown to the sex,

She rose with a smile from the ruins of her life, amidst which she had heart-brokenly sat down with all her things on.

"I knew you'd come back," she said.

"So did I," he answered. "I am much too good and noble to sacrifice my preference to my duty."

"I didn't care particularly for the two horses, Basil," she said, as they descended to the barouche. "It was your refusing them that hurt me."

"And I didn't want the one-horse carriage. It was your insisting so that provoked me."

"Do you think people *ever* quarrelled before on a wedding journey?" asked Isabel as they drove gaily out of the city.

"Never! I can't conceive of it. I suppose if this were written down, nobody would believe it."

"No, nobody could," said Isabel, musingly; and she added after a pause, "I wish you would tell me just what you thought of me, dearest. Did you feel as you did when our little affair was broken off, long ago? Did you hate me?"

"I did, most cordially; but not half so much as I despised myself the next moment. As to its being like a lover's quarrel, it wasn't. It was more bitter; so much more love than lovers ever give had to be taken back. Besides, it had no dignity, and a lover's quarrel always has. A lover's quarrel always springs from a more serious cause, and has an air of romantic tragedy. This had no grace of the kind. It was a poor shabby little squabble."

"O, don't call it so, Basil! I should like you to respect even a quarrel of ours more than that. It was tragical enough with me, for I didn't see how it could ever be made up. I knew *I* couldn't make the advances. I don't think it is quite feminine to be first to forgive, is it?"

"I'm sure I can't say. Perhaps it *would* be rather unladylike."

"Well you see, dearest, what I am trying to get at is this: whether we shall love each other the more or the less for it. *I* think we shall get on all the better for a while, on account of it. But I should have said it was totally out of character. It's something you might have expected of a very young bridal couple; but after what we've been through, it seems too improbable."

"Very well," said Basil, who, having made all the concessions, could not enjoy the quarrel as she did, simply because it was theirs; "let's behave as if it had never been."

"O no, we can't. To me, it's as if we had just won each other."

In fact it gave a wonderful zest and freshness to that ride round the mountain, and shed a beneficent glow upon the rest of their journey. The sun came out through the thin clouds, and lighted up the vast plain that swept away north and east, with the purple heights against the eastern sky. The royal mountain lifted its graceful mass beside them, and hid the city wholly from sight. Peasant-villages, in the shade of beautiful elms, dotted the plain in every direction, and at intervals crept up to the side of the road along which they drove. But these had been corrupted by a more ambitious architecture since Basil saw them last, and were no longer purely French in appearance. Then, nearly every house was a tannery in a modest way, and poetically published the fact by the display of a sheep's tail over the front door, like a bush at a wine-shop. Now, if the tanneries still existed, the poetry of the sheep's tails had vanished from the portals. But our friends were consoled by meeting numbers of the peasants jolting home from market in the painted carts, which are doubtless of the pattern of the carts first built there two hundred years ago. They were grateful for the immortal old women, crooked and brown with the labour of the fields, who abounded in these vehicles; when a huge girl jumped from the tail of her cart, and showed the thick, clumsy ankles of a true peasant-maid, they could only sigh out their unspeakable satisfaction.

Gardens embowered and perfumed the low cottages, through the open doors of which they could see the exquisite neatness of the life within. One of the doors opened into a school-house, where they beheld with rapture the school-mistress, book in hand, and with a quaint cap on her grey head, and encircled by her flock of little boys and girls.

By-and-by it began to rain again; and now while their driver stopped to put up the top of the barouche, they entered a country church which had taken their fancy, and walked up the aisle with the steps that blend with silence rather than break it, while they heard only the soft whisper of the shower without. There was no one there but themselves. The urn of holy water seemed not to have been troubled that day, and no penitent knelt at the shrine, before which twinkled so faintly one lighted lamp. The white roof swelled into dim arches over their heads; the pale day like a visible hush stole through

L

the painted windows; they heard themselves breathe as they crept from picture to picture.

A narrow door opened at the side of the high altar, and a slender young priest appeared in a long black robe, and with shaven head. He, too, as he moved with noiseless feet, seemed a part of the silence; and when he approached with dreamy black eyes fixed upon them, and bowed courteously, it seemed impossible he should speak. But he spoke, the pale young priest, the dark-robed tradition, the tonsured vision of an age and a church that are passing.

"Do you understand French, monsieur?

"A very little, monsieur."

"A very little is more than my English," he said, yet he politely went the round of the pictures with them, and gave them the names of the painters between his crossings at the different altars. At the high altar there was a very fair Crucifixion; before this the priest bent one knee. "Fine picture, fine altar, fine church," he said in English. At last they stopped near the poor-box. As their coins clinked against those within, he smiled serenely upon the good heretics. Then he bowed, and, as if he had relapsed into the past, he vanished through the narrow door by which he had entered.

Basil and Isabel stood speechless a moment on the church steps. Then she cried,—

"O, why *didn't* something happen?"

"Ah, my dear! what could have been half so good as the nothing that did happen? Suppose we knew him to have taken orders because of a disappointment in love: how common it would have made him; everybody has been crossed in love once or twice." He bade the driver take them back to the hotel. "This is the very *bouquet* of adventure: why should we care for the grosser body? I dare say if we knew all about yonder pale young priest, we should not think him half so interesting as we do now."

At dinner they spent the intervals of the courses in guessing the nationality of the different persons, and in wondering if the Canadians did not make it a matter of conscientious loyalty to out-English the English even in the matter of pale-ale and sherry, and in rotundity of person and freshness of face, just as they emulated them in the cut of their clothes and whiskers. Must they found even their health upon the health of the mother-country?

Our friends began to detect something servile in it all, and but that they were such amiable persons, the loyally perfect digestion of Montreal would have gone far to impair their own.

The loyalty, which had already appeared to them in the cathedral, suggested itself in many ways upon the street, when they went out after dinner to do that little shopping which Isabel had planned to do in Montreal. The bookseller's windows were full of Canadian editions of our authors, and English copies of English works, instead of our pirated editions; the dry-goods stores were gay with fabrics in the London taste and garments of the London shape; here was the sign of a photographer to the Queen, there of a hatter to H. R. H. the Prince of Wales, a barber was "under the patronage of H.R.H. the Prince of Wales, H. E. the Duke of Cambridge, and the gentry of Montreal." *Ich dien* was the motto of a restauranteur; a hosier had gallantly labelled his stock in trade with *Honi soit qui mal y pense.* Again they noted the English solidity of the civic edifices, and already they had observed in the foreign population a difference from that at home. They saw no German faces on the streets, and the Irish faces had not that truculence which they wear sometimes with us. They had not lost their native simpleness and kindliness; the Irishmen who drove the public carriages were as civil as our own Boston hackmen, and behaved as respectfully under the shadow of England here, as they would have done under it in Ireland. The problem which vexes us seems to have been solved pleasantly enough in Canada. Is it because the Celt cannot brook equality; and where he has not an established and recognized caste above him, longs to trample on those about him; and if he cannot be lowest, will at least be highest?

However our friends did not suffer this or any other advantage of the colonial relation to divert them from the opinion to which their observation was gradually bringing them,—that its overweening loyalty placed a great country like Canada in a very silly attitude, the attitude of an overgrown unmanly boy, clinging to the maternal skirts, and though spoilt and wilful, without any character of his own. The constant reference of local hopes to that remote centre beyond the seas, the test of success by the criterions of a necessarily different civilization, the social and intellectual dependence implied by traits that meet the most hurried glance in the Dominion, give an effect of meanness to the whole fabric. Doubtless it is a life of comfort, of peace, of irresponsibility they live there but it lacks the grandeur which no sum of material prosperity can give; it is ignoble, like all voluntarily subordinate things. Somehow, one feels that it has no basis in the New World, and that till it is shaken loose from England it cannot have.

It would be a pity, however, if it should be parted from the parent country merely to be joined to an unsympathetic half-brother like ourselves; and nothing, fortunately, seems to be further from the Canadian mind. There are some experiments no longer possible to us which could still be tried there to the advantage of civilization, and we were better two great nations side by side than a union of discordant traditions and ideas. But none the less does the American traveller swelling with forgetfulness of the shabby despots who govern New York, and the swindling railroad kings whose word is law to the whole land, feel like saying to the hulking young giant beyond St. Lawrence and the Lakes, "Sever the apron-strings of allegiance, and try to be yourself whatever you are."

Something of this sort Basil said, though of course not in apostrophic phrase, nor with Isabel's entire concurrence, when he explained to her that it was to the colonial dependence of Canada she owed the ability to buy things so cheaply there.

The fact is that the ladies' parlour at the hotel had been after dinner no better than a den of smugglers, in which the fair contrabandists had debated the best means of evading the laws of their country. At heart every man is a smuggler, and how much more every woman! She would have no scruple in ruining the silk and woollen interests throughout the United States. She is a free-trader by intuitive perception of right and is limited in practice by nothing but fear of the statute. What could be taken into the States without detection, was the subject before that wicked conclave; and next, what it would pay to buy in Canada. It seemed that silk umbrellas were most eligible wares; and in the display of such purchases the parlour was given the appearance of a violent thunder-storm. Gloves it was not advisable to get; they were better at home as were many kinds of fine woollen goods. But laces, which you could carry about you, were excellent; and so was any kind of silk. Could it be carried if simply cut, and not made up? There was a difference about this: the friend of one lady had taken home half a trunkful of cut silks; the friend of another had "run up the breadths" of one lone silk skirt, and then lost it by the rapacity of the customs officers. It was pretty much luck, and whether the officers happened to be in good-humor or not. You must not try to take in anything out of season, however. One had heard of a Boston lady going home in July, who "had the furs taken off her back," in that inclement month. Best get everything seasonable and put it on at once. "And then, you know, if they ask you, you can say it's been worn. To this black wisdom came the combined knowledge of those miscreants. Basil could not repress a shudder at the innate depravity of the female heart. Here were virgins nurtured in the most spotless purity of life, here were virtuous mothers of families, here were venerable matrons, patterns in society and the church,—smugglers to a woman, and eager for any guilty subterfuge! He glanced at Isabel to see what effect the evil conversation had upon her. Her eyes sparkled; her cheeks glowed; all the woman was on fire for smuggling. He sighed heavily and went out with her to do the little shopping.

Shall I follow them upon their excursion? Shopping in Montreal is very much what it is in Boston or New York, I imagine, except that the clerks have a more honeyed sweetness of manners towards the ladies of our nation, and are surprisingly generous constructionists of our revenue laws. Isabel had profited by every word that she had heard in the ladies' parlour, and she would not venture upon unsafe ground; but her tender eyes looked her unutterable longing to believe in the charming possibilities that the clerks suggested. She bemoaned herself before the corded silks, which there was no time to have made up; the piece-velvets and the linens smote her to the heart. But they also stimulated her invention, and she bought and bought of the made-up wares in real or fancied needs, till Basil represented that neither their purses nor their trunks could stand any more. "O, don't be troubled about the trunks, dearest," she cried, with that gaiety which nothing but shopping can kindle in a woman's heart; while he faltered on from counter to counter, wondering at which he should finally swoon from fatigue. At last, after she had declared repeatedly, "There, now, I *am* done," she briskly led the way back to the hotel to pack up her purchases.

Basil parted with her at the door. He was a man of high principle himself, and that scene in the smuggler's den, and his wife's preparation for transgression were revelations for which nothing could have consoled him but a paragon umbrella for five dollars, and an excellent business suit of Scotch goods for twenty.

When some hours later he sat with Isabel on the Quebec, and summed up the profits of their shopping, they were both in the kindliest mood towards the poor

Canadians, who had built the admirable city abode before them.

For miles the water-front of Montreal is superbly faced with quays and locks of solid stone masonry, and thus she is clean and beautiful to the very feet. Stately piles of architecture, instead of the foul old tumble-down warehouses that dishonour the waterside in most cities, rise from the broad wharves; behind these spring the twin towers of Notre Dame, and the steeples of the other churches above the city roofs.

"It's noble, yes, it's noble after the best that Europe can show," said Isabel, with enthusiasm; "and what a pleasant day we've had here! Doesn't even our quarrel show *couleur de rose* in this light?"

"One side of it," answered Basil, dreamily, "but all the rest is black."

"What do you mean, my dear?"

"Why, the Nelson Monument, with the sunset on it, at the head of the street there."

The effect was so fine that Isabel could not be angry with him for failing to heed what she had said and she mused a moment with him.

"It seems rather far-fetched," she said presently, "to erect a monument to Nelson in Montreal, doesn't it? But then, it's a very absurd monument when you're near it," she added, thoughtfully.

Basil did not answer at once for gazing on this Nelson column in Jacques Cartier Square, his thoughts wandered away, not to the hero of the Nile, but the doughty old Breton navigator, the first white man who ever set foot upon that shore, and who more than three hundred years ago explored the St. Lawrence as far as Montreal, and in the splendid autumn weather climbed to the top of her green height and named it. The scene that Jacques Cartier then beheld, like a mirage of the past projected upon the present, floated before him, and he saw at the mountain's foot the Indian city of Hochelaga, with its vast and populous lodges of bark, its encircling palisades, and its wide outlying fields of yellow maize. He heard with Jacques Cartier's sense the blare of his followers' trumpets down in the open square of the barbarous city, where the soldiers of many an Old-World fight, "with moustached lip and bearded chin, with arquebuse and glittering halberd, helmet, and cuirass," moved among the plumed and painted savages; then he lifted Jacques Cartier's eyes, and looked out upon the magnificent landscape. "East, west, and north, the mantling forest was over all, and the broad blue ribbon of the great river glistened amid a realm of verdure. Beyond to the bounds of Mexico, stretched a leafy desert, and the vast hive of industry, the mighty battle-ground of later centuries, lay sunk in savage torpor, wrapped in illimitable woods."

A vaguer picture of Champlain, who, seeking a westward route to China and the East, some three quarters of a century later, had fixed the first trading-post at Montreal, and camped upon the spot where the convent of the Grey Nuns now stands, appeared before him, and vanished with all its fleets of fur-traders' boats and hunters' birch canoes, and the watch-fires of both; and then in the sweet light of the spring morning, he saw Maisonneuve leaping ashore upon the green meadows, that spread all gay with early flowers where Hochelaga once stood, and with the black-robed Jesuits, the high-born, delicately nurtured, and devoted nuns, and the steel-clad soldiers of his train, kneeling about the altar raised there in the wilderness, and silent amidst the silence of nature at the lifted Host.

He painted a semblance of all this for Isabel, using the colours of the historian who has made these scenes the beautiful inheritance of all dreamers, and sketched the battles, the miracles, the sufferings, and the penances through which the pious colony was preserved and prospered, till they both grew impatient of modern Montreal, and would fain have had the ancient Villemarie back in its place.

"Think of Maisonneuve, dearest, climbing in midwinter to the top of the mountain there, under a heavy cross set with the bones of saints, and planting it on the summit, in fulfilment of a vow to do so if Villemarie were saved from the freshet; and then of Madame de la Peltrie romantically receiving the sacrament there, while all Villemarie fell down adoring! Ah, that was a picturesque people! When did ever a Boston governor climb to the top of Beacon hill in fulfilment of a vow? To be sure, we may yet see a New York governor doing something of the kind—if he can find a hill. But this ridiculous column to Nelson, who never had anything to do with Montreal," he continued; "it really seems to me the perfect expression of snobbish colonial dependence and sentimentality, seeking always to identify itself with the mother-country, and ignoring the local past and its heroic figures. A column to Nelson in Jacques Cartier Square, on the ground that was trodden by Champlain, and won for its present masters by the death of Wolfe!"

The boat departed on her trip to Quebec. During
supper they were served by French waiters, who, without apparent English of their own, miraculously understood that of the passengers, except in the case of the
furious gentleman who wanted English breakfast tea;
to so much English as that their inspiration did not
reach, and they forced him to compromise on coffee. It
was a French boat, owned by a French company, and
seemed to be officered by Frenchmen throughout; certainly, as our tourists in the joy of their good appetites
affirmed, the cook was of that culinarily delightful nation.

The boat was almost as large as those of the Hudson,
but it was not so lavishly splendid, though it had everything that could minister to the comfort and self-respect
of the passengers. These were of all nations, but chiefly
Americans, with some French Canadians. The former
gathered on the forward promenade, enjoying what little
of the landscape the growing night left visible, and the
latter made society after their manner in the saloon. They
were plain-looking men and women, mostly, and provincial, it was evident, to their inmost hearts; provincial
in origin, provincial by inheritance, by all their circumstances, social and political. Their relation with France
was not a proud one, but it was not like submersion by
the slip-slop of English colonial loyalty; yet they seem
to be troubled by no memories of their hundred years'
dominion of the land that they rescued from the wilderness, and that was wrested from them by war. It is a
strange fate for any people thus to have been cut off
from the parent-country, and abandoned to whatever
destiny their conquerors chose to reserve for them; and
if each of the race wore the sadness and strangeness of

that fate in his countenance it would not be wonderful. Perhaps it is wonderful that none of them show anything of the kind. In their desertion they have multiplied and prospered; they may have a national grief, but they hide it well; and probably they have none.

Later, one of them appeared to Isabel in the person of the pale, slender young ecclesiastic who had shown her and Basil the pictures in the country church. She was confessing to the priest, and she was not at all surprised to find that he was Basil in a suit of mediæval armour. He had an immense cross on his shoulder.

"To get this cross to the top of the mountain," thought Isabel, "we must have two horses. Basil," she added, aloud, "we must have two horses!"

"Ten, if you like, my dear," answered his voice, cheerfully, "though I think we'd better ride up in the omnibus."

She opened her eyes, and saw him smiling. "We're in sight of Quebec," he said. "Come out as soon as you can, —come out into the seventeenth century."

IX.

ISABEL hurried out upon the forward promenade, where all the other passengers seemed to be assembled, and beheld a vast bulk of grey and purple rock, swelling two hundred feet up from the mists of the river, and taking the early morning light warm upon its face and crown. Black-hulked, red-chimneyed Liverpool steamers, gay river-craft and ships of every sail and flag, filled the stream athwart which the ferries sped their swift traffic-laden shuttles; a lower town clung to the foot of the rock, and crept, populous and picturesque, up its side; from the massive citadel on its crest flew the red banner of Saint George, and along its brow swept the grey wall of the famous, heroic, beautiful city, overtopped by many a gleaming spire and antique roof.

Slowly out of our work-day, business-suited, modern world the vessel steamed up to this city on an olden time and another ideal,—to her who was a lady from the first, devout and proud and strong, and who still, after two hundred and fifty years, keeps perfect the image and memory of the feudal past from which she sprung. Upon her height she sits unique; and when you say Quebec, having once beheld her, you invoke a sense of mediæval strangeness and of beauty which the name of no other city could intensify.

179

As they drew near the steamboat wharf they saw, swarming over the broad square, a market beside which the Bonsecours Market would have shown as common as the Quincy, and up the odd wooden side-walked street stretched an aisle of carriages and those high swung calashes, which are to Quebec what the gondolas are to Venice. But the hand of destiny was upon our tourists, and they rode up town in an omnibus. They were going to the dear old Hotel Musty in ——— Street, wanting which Quebec is not to be thought of without a pang. It is now closed, and Prescott Gate, through which they drove into the Upper Town, has been demolished since the summer of last year. Swiftly whirled along the steep winding road, by those Quebec horses which expect to gallop up hill whatever they do going down, they turned a corner of the towering weed-grown rock, and shot in under the low arch of the gate, pierced with smaller doorways for the foot-passengers. The gloomy masonry dripped with damp, the doors were thickly studded with heavy spikes; old cannon, thrust endwise into the ground at the sides of the gate, protected it against passing wheels. Why did not some semi-forbidding commissary of police, struggling hard to overcome his native politeness, appear and demand their passports? The illusion was otherwise perfect, and it needed but this touch. How often in the adored Old World, which we so love and disapprove, had they driven in through such gates at that morning hour! On what perverse pretext, then was it not some ancient town of Normandy?

"Put a few enterprising Americans in here, and they'd soon rattle this old wall down and let in a little fresh

air!" said a patriotic voice at Isabel's elbow, and continued to find fault with the narrow, irregular streets,
the huddling gables, the quaint roofs, through which and
under which they drove on to the hotel.

As they dashed into a broad open square, "Here is the
French Cathedral; there is the Upper Town Market;
yonder are the Jesuit Barracks!" cried Basil; and they
had a passing glimpse of grey stone towers at one side
of the square, and a low, massive yellow building at the
other, and, between the two, long ranks of carts, and
fruit and vegetable stands, protected by canvas awnings
and broad umbrellas. Then they dashed round the corner
of a street, and drew up before the hotel door.   The low
ceilings, the thick walls, the clumsy wood-work, the
wandering corridors, gave the hotel all the desired character of age, and its slovenly state bestowed an additional
charm.   In another place they might have demanded
neatness, but in Quebec they would almost have resented
it.   By a chance they had the best room in the house, but
they held it only till certain people who had engaged it
by telegraph should arrive in the hourly expected
steamer from Liverpool; and moreover, the best room at
Hotel Musty was consolingly bad.   The house was very
full, and the Ellisons (who had come on with them
from Montreal) were bestowed in less state only on like
conditions.

The travellers all met at breakfast, which was ad-
mirably cooked, and well served, with the attendance
of those swarms of flies which infest Quebec, and especially infested the old Musty House, in summer.   It
had, of course, the attraction of broiled salmon, upon
which the traveller breakfasts every day as long as he

remains in Lower Canada; and it represented the abundance of wild berries in the Quebec market; and it was otherwise a breakfast worthy of the appetites that honoured it.

There were not many other Americans besides themselves at this hotel, which seemed, indeed, to be kept open to oblige such travellers as had been there before, and could not persuade themselves to try the new Hotel St. Louis, whither the vastly greater number resorted. Most of the faces our tourists saw were English or English-Canadian, and the young people from Omaha, who had got here by some chance, were scarcely in harmony with the place. They appeared to be a bridal party, but which of the two sisters, in buff linen clad from head to foot, was the bride, never became known. Both were equally free with the husband, and he was impartially fond of both: it was quite a family affair.

For a moment Isabel harboured the desire to see the city in company with Miss Ellison; but it was only a passing weakness. She remembered directly the coolness between friends which she had seen caused by objects of interest in Europe, and she wisely deferred a more intimate acquaintance till it could have a purely social basis. After all, nothing is so tiresome as continual exchange of sympathy, or so apt to end in mutual dislike,— except gratitude. So the ladies parted friends till dinner, and drove off in separate carriages.

As in other show cities, there is a routine at Quebec for travellers who come on Saturday and go on Monday, and few depart from it. Our friends necessarily, therefore, drove first to the citadel. It was raining one of those cold rains by which the scarce-banished winter re-

minds the Canadian fields of his nearness even in mid-summer, though between the bitter showers the air was sultry and close; and it was just the light in which to see the grim strength of the fortress next strongest to Gibraltar in the world. They passed a heavy iron gateway, and up through a winding lane of masonry to the gate of the citadel, where they were delivered into the care of Private Joseph Drakes, who was to show them such parts of the place as are open to curiosity. But, a citadel which has never stood a siege, or been threatened by any danger more serious than Fenianism, soon becomes, however strong, but a dull piece of masonry to the civilian; and our tourists more rejoiced in the crumbling fragment of the old French wall which the English destroyed than in all they had built; and they valued the latter work chiefly for the glorious prospects of the St. Lawrence and its mighty valleys which it commanded. Advanced into the centre of an amphitheatre inconceivably vast, that enormous beak of rock overlooks the narrow angle of the river, and then, in every direction, immeasurable stretches of gardened vale, and wooded upland, till all melts into the purple of the encircling mountains. Far and near are lovely white villages nestling under elms, in the heart of fields and meadows; and everywhere the long, narrow, accurately divided farms stretch downward to the river-shores. The best roads on the continent make this beauty and richness accessible; each little village boasts some natural wonder in stream, or lake, or cataract: and this landscape, magnificent beyond any in eastern America, is historical and interesting beyond all others. Hither came Jacques Cartier three hundred and fifty years ago, and wintered on the
M

low point there by the St. Charles; here, nearly a century after, but still fourteen years before the landing at Plymouth, Champlain founded the missionary city of Quebec; round this rocky beak came sailing the half-piratical armament of the Calvinist Kirks in 1629, and seized Quebec in the interest of the English, holding it three years; in the Lower Town, yonder, first landed the coldly welcomed Jesuits, who came with the returning French, and made Quebec for ever eloquent of their zeal, their guile, their heroism; at the foot of this rock lay the fleet of Sir William Phipps, governor of Massachusetts, and vainly assailed it in 1698; in 1759 came Wolfe, and embattled all the region, on river and land, till at last the bravely defended city fell into his dying hand on the Plains of Abraham; here Montgomery laid down his life at the head of the boldest and most hopeless effort of our War of Independence.

Private Joseph Drake, with the generosity of an enemy expecting drink-money, pointed out the sign-board on the face of the craig commemorating Montgomery's death; and then showed them the officers' quarters and those of the common soldiers, not far from which was a line of hang-dog fellows drawn up to receive sentence for divers small misdemeanours, from an officer whose blonde whiskers drooped Dundrearily from his fresh English cheeks. There was that immense difference between him and the men in physical grandeur and beauty, which is so notable in the aristocratically ordered military services of Europe, and which makes the rank seem of another race from the file. Private Drakes saluted his superior, and visibly deteriorated in his presence, though his breast was covered with medals, and he had fought

England's battles in every part of the world.   It was a
gross injustice, the triumph of a thousand years of
wrong; and it was touching to have Private Drakes say
that he expected in three months to begin life for himself, after twenty years' service of the Queen; and did
they think he could get anything to do in the States? He
scarcely knew what he was fit for, but he thought—to so
little in him came the victories he had helped to win in
the Crimea, in China, and in India—that he could take
care of a gentleman's horse and work about his place.
He looked inquiringly at Basil, as if he might be a
gentleman with a horse to be taken care of and a place to
be worked about, and made him regret that he was not a
man of substance enough to provide for Private Drakes
and Mrs. Drakes and the brood of Ducklings, who had
been shown to him stowed away in one of those cavernous
rooms in the earthworks where the married soldiers have
their quarters.   His regret enriched the reward of
Private Drakes' service,—which perhaps answered one of
Private Drakes' purposes, if not his chief aim.   He
promised to come to the States upon the pressing advice
of Isabel, who, speaking from her own large experience,
declared that everybody got on there; and he bade our
friends an affectionate farewell as they drove away to the
Plains of Abraham.

The fashionable suburban cottages and places of Quebec are on the St. Louis Road leading northward to the
old battle-ground and beyond it; but these face chiefly
towards the river St. Lawrence and St. Charles, and
lofty hedges and shrubbery hide them in an English
seclusion from the highway; so that the visitor may un-
interruptedly meditate whatever emotion he will for the

scene of Wolfe's death as he rides along. His loftiest
emotion will want the noble height of that heroic soul,
who must always stand forth in history a figure of beautiful and singular distinction, admirable alike for the sensibility and daring, the poetic pensiveness, and the martial
ardour that mingled in him and taxed his feeble frame
with tasks greater than it could bear. The whole story
of the capture of Quebec is full of romantic splendour
and pathos. Her fall was a triumph for all the Eng-
lish-speaking race, and to us Americans, long scourged
by the cruel Indian wars plotted within her walls or
sustained by her strength, such a blessing as was hailed
with ringing bells and blazing bonfires throughout the
Colonies; yet now we cannot think without pity of the
hopes extinguished and the labours brought to naught in
her overthrow. That strange colony of priests and
soldiers, of martyrs and heroes, of which she was the
capital, willing to perish for an allegiance to which the
mother-country was indifferent, and fighting against the
armies with which England was prepared to outnumber
the whole Canadian population, is a magnificent
spectacle; and Montcalm lying down his life to lose Quebec is not less affecting than Wolfe dying to win her. The
heart opens towards the soldier who recited, on the eve
of his costly victory, the "Elegy in a Country Churchyard," which he would "rather have written than beat
the French to-morrow;" but it aches for the defeated
general, who, hurt to death, answered, when told how
brief his time was, "So much the better; then I shall not
live to see the surrender of Quebec."

In the city for which they perished their fame has
never been divided. The English have shown them-

selves very generous victors; perhaps nothing could be alleged against them, but that they were victors. A shaft common to Wolfe and Montcalm celebrates them both in the Governor's Garden; and in the Chapel of the Ursuline Convent a tablet is placed, where Montcalm died, by the same conquerors who raised to Wolfe's memory the column on the battlefield.

A dismal prison covers the grounds where the hero fell, and the monument stands on the spot where Wolfe breathed his last, on ground lower than the rest of the field; the friendly hollow that sheltered him from the fire of the French dwarfs his monument; yet it is sufficient, and the simple inscription, "Here died Wolfe victorious," gives it a dignity which many cubits of added stature could not bestow. Another of those bitter showers, which had interspersed the morning sunshine, drove suddenly across the open plain, and our tourists comfortably sentimentalized the scene behind the close-drawn curtains of their carriage. Here a whole empire had been lost and won, Basil reminded Isabel; and she said, "Only think of it!" and looked to a wandering fold of her skirt, upon which the rain beat through a rent of the curtain.

Do I pitch the pipe too low? We poor honest men are at a sad disadvantage; and now and then I am minded to give a loose to fancy, and attribute something really grand and fine to my people, in order to make them worthier the reader's respected acquaintance. But again, I forbid myself in a higher interest; and I am afraid that even if I were less victorious, I could not exalt their mood upon a battle-field; for of all things of the past a battle is the least conceivable. I have heard men who fought in many battles say that the recollec-

tion was like a dream to them; and what can the merely
civilian imagination do on the Plains of Abraham, with
the fact that there, more than a century ago, certain
thousands of Frenchmen marched out, on a bright September morning, to kill and maim as many Englishmen?
This ground, so green and soft with grass beneath the
feet, was it once torn with shot and soaked with the blood
of men? Did they lie here in ranks and heaps, the
miserable slain, for whom tender hearts away yonder
over the sea were to ache and break? Did the wretches
that fell wounded stretch themselves here, and writhe
beneath the feet of friend and foe, or crawl away for
shelter into little hollows, and behind bushes and fallen
trees? Did he, whose soul was so full of noble and
sublime impulses, die here, shot through like some ravening beast? The loathsome carnage, the shrieks, the
hellish din of arms, the cries of victory,—I vainly strive
to conjure up some image of it all now; and God be
thanked, horrible spectre! that, fill the world with sorrow as thou wilt, thou still remainest incredible in its
moments of sanity and peace. Least credible art thou
on the old battle-fields, where the mother of the race
denies thee with breeze and sun and leaf and bird, and
every blade of grass! The red stain in Basil's thought
yielded to the rain sweeping across the pasture-land
from which it had long since faded, and the words on the
monument, "Here died Wolfe victorious," did not pro-
claim his bloody triumph over the French, but his self-
conquest, his victory over fear and pain and love of
life. Alas! when shall the poor, blind, stupid world
honour those who renounce self in the joy of their kind,
equally with those who devote themselves through the

anguish and loss of thousands? So old a world, and groping still!

The tourists were better fitted for the next occasion of sentiment, which was at the Hotel Dieu, whither they went after returning from the battle-field. It took all the mal-address of which travellers are masters to secure admittance, and it was not till they had rung various wrong bells, and misunderstood many soft nun-voices speaking French through grated doors, and set divers sympathetic spectators doing ineffectual services, that they at last found the proper entrance, and were answered in English that the porter would ask if they might see the chapel. They hoped to find there the skull of Brébeuf, one of those Jesuit martyrs who perished long ago for the conversion of a race that has perished, and whose relics they had come, fresh from their reading of Parkman, with some vague and patronizing intention to revere. An elderly sister with a pale, kind face led them through a ward of the hospital into the chapel, which they found in the expected taste, and exquisitely neat and cool, but lacking the martyr's skull. They asked if it were not to be seen. "Ah, yes, poor Père Brébeuf!" sighed the gentle sister, with the tone and manner of having lost him yesterday; "we had it down only last week, showing it to some Jesuit fathers; but it's in the convent now, and isn't to be seen." And there mingled apparently in her regret for Père Brébeuf a confusing sense of his actual state as a portable piece of furniture. She would not let them praise the chapel. It was very clean, but there was nothing to see in it. She deprecated their compliments with many shrugs, but she was pleased; for when we renounce the pomps and vanities of this world, we are pretty sure to find them in some other,—if we are women. She, good and pure soul, whose whole life was given to self-denying toil, had yet something angelically coquettish in her manner, a spiritual-worldliness which was the clarified likeness of this worldliness. O, had they seen the Hôtel Dieu at Montreal? Then (with a vivacious wave of the hands) they would not care to look at this, which by comparison was nothing. Yet she invited them to go through the wards if they would, and was clearly proud to have them see the wonderful cleanness and comfort of the place. There were not many patients, but here and there a wan or fevered face looked at them from its pillow, or a weak form drooped beside a bed, or a group of convalescents softly talked together. They came presently to the last hall, at the end of which sat another nun, beside a window that gave a view of the busy port, and beyond it the landscape of village-lit plain and forest-darkened height. On a table at her elbow stood a rose-tree, on which hung two only pale tea-roses, so fair, so perfect, that Isabel cried out in wonder and praise. Ere she could prevent it, the nun, to whom there had been some sort of presentation, gathered one of the roses, and with a shy grace offered it to Isabel, who shrank back a little as from too costly a gift. "Take it," said the first nun, with her pretty French accent; while the other, who spoke no English at all, beamed a placid smile; and Isabel took it. The flower, lying light in her palm, exhaled a delicate odour, and a thrill of exquisite compassion for it trembled through her heart, as if it had been the white, cloistered life of the silent nun; with its pallid loveliness, it was as a flower that had taken the veil. It could never have uttered the burning passion of a lover for his mistress; the nightingale could have found no thorn on it to press his aching poet's heart against; but sick and weary eyes had dwelt gratefully upon it; at most it might have expressed, like a prayer, the nun's stainless love of some favourite saint in paradise. Cold, and pale and sweet,— was it indeed only a flower, this cloistered rose of the Hôtel Dieu?

"Breathe it," said the gentle Grey Sister; "sometimes the air of the hospital offends. Not us, we are used; but you come from the outside." And she gave her rose for this humble use as lovingly as she devoted herself to her lowly cares.

"It is very little to see," she said at the end; "but if you are pleased, I am very glad. Good-bye, good-bye!" She stood with her arms folded, and watched them out of sight with her kind, coquettish little smile, and then the mute, blank life of the nun resumed her.

From Hôtel Dieu to Hotel Musty it was but a step; both were in the same street; but our friends fancied themselves to have come an immense distance when they sat down at an early dinner, amidst the clash of crockery and cutlery, and looked round upon all the profane travelling world assembled. Their regard presently fixed upon one company which monopolized a whole table, and were defined from the other diners by peculiarities as marked as those of the Sœurs Grises themselves. They were only two men among some eight or ten women; one of the former had a bad amiable face, with eyes full of a merry deviltry; the other, clean-shaven, and dark, was demure and silent as a priest. The ladies were of various types, but of one effect, with large rolling eyes, and faces that somehow regarded the be-

holder as from a distance, and with an impartial feeling
for him as for an element of publicity. One of them,
who caressed a lap-dog with one hand while she served
herself with the other, was, as she seemed to believe, a
blonde; she had pale blue eyes, and her hair was cut in
front so as to cover her forehead with a straggling sandy-
coloured fringe. She had an English look, and three or
four others, with dark complexions and black, unsteady
eyes, and various *abandon* of back-hair, looked like
Cockney houris of Jewish blood; while two of the lovely
company were clearly of our own nation, as was the
young man with the reckless laughing face. The ladies
were dressed and jewelled with a kind of broad effective-
ness, which was to the ordinary style of society what
scene-painting is to painting, and might have borne close
inspection no better. They seemed the best-humoured
people in the world, and on the kindliest terms with each
other. The waiters shared their pleasant mood, and
served them affectionately, and were now and then invited to join in the gay talk which babbled on over dis-
located aspirates, and filled the air with a sentiment of
vagabond enjoyment, of the romantic freedom of violated
convention, of something Gil Blas-like, almost picaresque.

If they had needed explanation it would have been
given by the announcement in the office of the hotel that
a troupe of British blondes was then appearing in Quebec for one week only.

After dinner they took possession of the parlour, and
while one strummed fitfully upon the ailing hotel piano,
the rest talked, and talked shop, of course, as all of us do
when several of a trade are got together.

"W'at," said the eldest of the dark-faced, black-haired

British blondes of Jewish race,—"w'at are we going to give at Montrehal?"

"We're going to give 'Pygmalion' at Montrehal," answered the British blonde of American birth, good-humouredly burlesquing the erring *h* of her sister.

"But we cahn't, you know," said the lady with the fringed forehead; "Hagnes is gone on to New York, and there's nobody to do Wenus."

"Yes, you know," demanded the first speaker, "oo's to do Wenus?"

"Bella's to do Wenus," said a third.

There was an outcry at this, and "Ow ever would she get herself up for Wenus?" and "W'at a guy she'll look!" and "Nonsense! Bella's too 'eavy for Wenus!" came from different lively critics; and the debate threatened to become too intimate for the public ear, when one of their gentlemen came in and said, "Charley don't seem so well this afternoon." On this the chorus changed its note, and at the proposal, "Poor Charley, let's go and cheer 'im hup a bit," the whole good-tempered company trooped out of the parlour together.

Our tourists meant to give the rest of the afternoon to that sort of aimless wandering to and fro about the streets which seizes a foreign city unawares, and best develops its charm of strangeness. So they went out and took their fill of Quebec with appetites keen through long fasting from the quaint and old, and only sharpened by Montreal, and impartially rejoiced in the crooked up-and-down hill streets; the thoroughly French domestic architecture of a place that thus denied having been English for a hundred years; the *porte-cochères* beside every house; the French names upon the doors, and the oddity of the bell-pulls; the rough-paved rattling streets; the shining roofs of tin, and the universal dormer-windows; the littleness of the private houses, and the greatness of the high-walled and garden-girdled convents; the breadths of weather-stained city wall, and the shaggy cliff beneath; the batteries, with their guns peacefully staring through loop-holes of masonry, and the red-coated sergeants flirting with nursery-maids upon the carriages, while the children tumbled about over the pyramids of shot and shell; the sloping market-place before the cathedral, where yet some remnant of the morning's traffic lingered under canvas canopies, and where Isabel bought a bouquet of marigolds and asters of an old woman peasant enough to have sold it in any market-place of Europe; the small, dark shops beyond the quarter invaded by English retail trade; the movement of all the strange figures of cleric and lay and military life; the sound of a foreign speech prevailing over the English; the encounter of other tourists, the passage back and forth through the different city gates; the public wooden stairways, dropping flight after flight from the Upper to the Lower Town; the bustle of the port, with its commerce and shipping and seafaring life huddled close in under the hill; the many desolate streets of the Lower Town, as black and ruinous as the last great fire left them; and the marshy meadows beyond, memorable of Recollets and Jesuits, of Cartier and Montcalm.

They went to the chapel of the Seminary at Laval University, and admired the Le Brun, and the other paintings of less merit, but equal interest through their suggestion of a whole dim religious world of paintings;

and then they spent half an hour in the cathedral, not so much in looking at the Crucifixion by Vandyck which is there, as in revelling amid the familiar *rococo* splendours of the temple. Every swaggering statue of a saint, every rope-dancing angel, every cherub of those that on the carven and gilded clouds above the high altar float--

"Like little wanton boys that swim on bladders,"—

was precious to them; the sacristan dusting the sacred properties with a feather brush, and giving each shrine a business-like nod as he passed, was as a long-lost brother; they had hearts of aggressive tenderness for the hour's devotion, and for the men with bourgeois or peasant faces, who stole a moment from affairs and crops, and gave it to the saints. There was nothing in the place that need remind them of America, and its taste was exactly that of a thousand other churches of the eighteenth century. They could easily have believed themselves in the furthest Catholic South, but for the two great porcelain stoves that stood in either side of the nave near the entrance, and that too vividly reminded them of the possibility of cold.

In fact, Quebec is a little painful in this and other confusions of the South and North, and one never quite reconciles himself to them. The Frenchmen, who expected to find there the climate of their native land, and ripen her wines in as kindly a sun, have perpetuated the image of home in so many things, that it goes to the heart with a painful emotion to find the sad, oblique light of the North upon them. As you ponder some characteristic aspect of Quebec,—a bit of street with heavy stone houses, opening upon a stretch of the city

wall, with a Lombardy poplar rising slim against it,—
you say, to your satisfied soul, "Yes, it is the real thing!"
and then all at once a sense of that Northern sky strikes
in upon you, and makes the reality a mere picture. The
sky is blue, the sun is often fiercely hot; you could not
perhaps prove that the pathetic radiance is not an
efflux of your own consciousness that summer is but
hanging over the land, briefly poising on wings which
flit at the first dash of rain, and will soon vanish in long
retreat before the snow. But somehow, from without or
from within, that light of the North is there.

It lay saddest, our travellers thought, upon the little
circular garden near Durham Terrace, where every
brightness of fall flowers abounded,—marigold, coxcomb,
snap-dragon, dahlia, hollyhock, and sunflower. It was a
substantial and hardy efflorescence, and they fancied that
fainter-hearted plants would have pined away in that
garden, where the little fountain, leaping up into the
joyless light, fell back again with a musical shiver. The
consciousness of this latent cold, of winter only held in
abeyance by the bright sun, was not deeper even in the
once magnificent, now neglected Governor's Garden,
where there was actually a rawness in the late afternoon
air, and whither they were strolling for the view from its
height, and to pay their duty to the obelisk raised there
to the common fame of Wolfe and Montcalm. The
sounding Latin inscription celebrates the royal governor-
general who erected it almost as much as the heroes to
whom it was raised; but these spectators did not be-
grudge the space given to his praise, for so fine a thought
merited praise. It enforced again the idea of a kind
of posthumous friendship between Wolfe and Montcalm,

which gives their memory its rare distinction, and unites them, who fell in fight against each other, as closely as if they had both died for the same cause.

Some lasting dignity seems to linger about the city that has once been a capital; and this odour of fallen nobility belongs to Quebec, which was a capital in the European sense, with all the advantages of a small vice-regal court, and its social and political intrigues, in the French times. Under the English, for a hundred years it was the centre of Colonial civilization and refinement, with a governor-general's residence and a brilliant, easy, and delightful society, to which the large garrison of former days gave gaiety and romance. The honours of a capital, first shared with Montreal and Toronto, now rest with half-savage Ottawa; and the garrison has dwindled to a regiment of rifles, whose presence would hardly be known, but for the natty sergeants lounging, stick in hand, about the streets and courting the nurse-maids. But in the days of old there were scenes of carnival pleasure in the Governor's Garden, and there the garrison band still plays once a week, when it is filled by the fashion and beauty of Quebec, and some semblance of the past is recalled. It is otherwise a lonesome, indifferently tended place, and on this afternoon there was no one there but a few loafing young fellows of low degree, French and English, and children that played screaming from seat to seat and path to path and over the too-heavily shaded grass. In spite of a conspicuous warning that any dog entering the garden would be destroyed, the place was thronged with dogs unmolested and apparently in no danger of the threatened doom. The seal of a disagreeable desolation was given in the

legend rudely carved upon one of the benches, "Success
to the Irish Republic!"

The morning of the next day our tourists gave to hearing mass at the French cathedral, which was not different, to their heretical senses, from any other mass,
except that the ceremony was performed with a very full
clerical force, and was attended by an uncommonly
devout congregation. With Europe constantly in their
minds, they were bewildered to find the worshippers not
chiefly old and young women, but men also of all ages
and of every degree, from the neat peasant in his Sab-
bath-day best to the modish young Quebecker, who
spread his handkerchief on the floor to save his pantaloons during the supplication. There was fashion and
education in large degree among the men, and there was
in all a pious attention to the function in poetical keeping with the origin and history of a city which the zeal
of the Church had founded.

A magnificent beadle, clothed in a gold-laced coat and
bearing a silver staff, bowed to them when they entered,
and, leading them to a pew, punched up a kneeling
peasant, who mutely resumed his prayers in the aisle
outside, while they took his place.   It appeared to
Isabel very unjust that their curiosity should displace
his religion; but she consoled herself by making Basil
give a shilling to the man who, preceded by the shining
beadle, came round to take up a collection. The peasant
could have given nothing but copper, and she felt that
this restored the lost balance of righteousness in their
favour. There was a sermon, very sweetly and grace-
fully delivered by a young priest of singular beauty,
even among clergy whose good looks are so notable as

those of Quebec; and then they followed the orderly
crowd of worshippers out, and left the cathedral to the
sacristan and the odour of incense.

They thought the type of French-Canadian better here
than at Montreal, and they particularly noticed the
greater number of pretty young girls. All classes were
well dressed; for though the best dressed could not be
called stylish according to the American standard, as
Isabel decided, and had only a provincial gentility, the
poorest wore garments that were clean and whole. Everybody, too, was going to have a hot Sunday dinner, if
there was any truth in the odours that steamed out of
every door and window; and this dinner was to be
abundantly garnished with onions, for the dullest nose
could not err concerning that savour.

Numbers of tourists, of a nationality that showed itself superior to every distinction of race, were strolling
vaguely, and not always quite happily about; but they
made no impression on the proper local character, and
the air throughout the morning was full of the sentiment
of Sunday in a Catholic city. There was the apparently
meaningless jangling of bells, with profound hushes between, and then more jubilant jangling, and then deeper
silence; there was the devout trooping of the crowds to
the churches; and there was the beginning of the long
afternoon's lounging and amusement with which the
people of that faith reward their morning's devotion.
Little stands for the sale of knotty apples and choke-
cherries and cakes and cider sprang magically into existence after service, and people were already eating and
drinking at them. The carriage-drivers resumed their
chase of the tourists, and the unvoiceful stir of the new

N

week had begun again.   Quebec, in fact, is but a pan-
tomimic reproduction of France; it is as if two centuries
in a new land, amidst the primeval silences of nature
and the long hush of the Northern winters, had stilled the
tongues of the lively folk and made them taciturn as we
of a graver race.   They have kept the ancestral vivacity
of manner; the elegance of the shrug is intact; the talking hands take part in dialogue; the agitated person will
have its share of expression. But the loud and eager tone
is wanting, and their dumb show mystifies the beholder
almost as much as the Southern architecture under the
slanting Northern sun.   It is not America; if it is not
France, what is it?

Of the many beauutiful things to see in the neighbourhood of Quebec, our wedding-journeyers were in doubt on
which to bestow their one precious afternoon.   Should it
be Lorette, with its cataract and its remnant of bleached
and fading Hurons, or the Isle of Orleans with its fertile
farms and its primitive peasant life, or Montmorenci,
with the unrivalled fall and the long drive through the
beautiful village of Beauport?   Isabel chose the last, because Basil had been there before, and it had to it the
poetry of the wasted years in which she did not know
him.   She had possessed herself of the journal of his
early travels, among the other portions and parcels re-
coverable from the dreadful past, and from time to time
on this journey she had read him passages out of it,
with mingled sentiment and irony, and, whether she was
mocking or admiring, equally to his confusion.   Now, as
they smoothly bowled away from the city, she made him
listen to what he had written of the same excursion long
ago.

It was, to be sure, a sad farrago of sentiment about the village and the rural sights, and especially a girl tossing hay in the field. Yet it had touches of nature and realty, and Basil could not utterly despise himself for having written it. "Yes," he said, "life was then a thing to be put into pretty periods; now it's something that has risks and averages, and may be insured."

There was regret, fancied or expressed, in his tone that made her sigh, "Ah! if I'd only had a *little* more money, you might have devoted yourself to literature;" for she was a true Bostonian in her honour of our poor craft.

"O, you're not greatly to blame," answered her husband, "and I forgive you the little wrong you've done me. I was quits with the Muse, at any rate, you know, before we were married; and I'm very well satisfied to go back to my applications and policies to-morrow."

To-morrow? The word struck cold upon her. Then their wedding journey would begin to end to-morrow! So it would, she owned with another sigh; and yet it seemed impossible.

"There, ma'am," said the driver, rising from his seat and facing round, while he pointed with his whip towards Quebec, "that's what we call the Silver City."

They looked back with him at the city, whose thousands of tinned roofs, rising one above the other from the water's edge to the citadel, were all a splendour of argent light in the afternoon sun. It was indeed as if some magic had clothed that huge rock, base and steepy flank and crest, with a silver city. They gazed upon the marvel with cries of joy that satisfied the driver's utmost pride in it, and Isabel said, "To live there, there in that Silver City, in perpetual sojourn! To be always going to go on a morrow that never came! To be for ever within one day of the end of a wedding journey that never ended!"

From far down the river by which they rode came the sound of a cannon, breaking the Sabbath repose of the air. "That's the gun of the Liverpool steamer, just coming in," said the driver.

"O," cried Isabel, "I'm thankful we're only to stay one night more, for now we shall be turned out of our nice room by those people who telegraphed for it!"

There is a continuous village along the St. Lawrence from Quebec, almost to Montmorenci; and they met crowds of villagers coming from the church as they passed through Beauport. But Basil was dismayed at the change that had befallen them. They had their Sunday's best on, and the women, instead of wearing the peasant costume in which he had first seen them, were now dressed as if out of "Harper's Bazaar" of the year before. He anxiously asked the driver if the broad straw hats and the bright sacks and kirtles were no more. "O, you'd see them on week-days, sir," was the answer, "but they're not so plenty any time as they used to be." He opened his store of facts about the *habitans*, whom he praised for every virtue,—for thrift, for sobriety, for neatness, for amiability; and his words ought to have had the greater weight, because he was of the Irish race, between which and the Canadians there is no kindness lost. But the looks of the passers-by corroborated him, and as for the little houses, open-doored beside the way, with the pleasant faces at window and portal, they were miracles of picturesqueness and cleanliness. From each the owner's slim domain, narrowing at every successive division among the abundant generations, runs back to hill or

river in well-defined lines, and beside the cottage is a
garden of pot-herbs, bordered with a flame of bright
autumn flowers; somewhere in decent seclusion grunts
the fattening pig, which is to enrich all those peas and
onions for the winter's broth; there is a cheerfulness of
poultry about the barns; I dare be sworn there is always
a small girl driving a flock of decorous ducks down the
middle of the street; and of the priest with a book under
his arm, passing a way-side shrine, what possible doubt?
The houses, which are of one model, are built by the
peasants themselves with the stone which their land
yields more abundantly than any other crop, and are
furnished with galleries and balconies to catch every ray
of the fleeting summer, and perhaps to remember the
long-lost ancestral summers of Normandy. At every
moment, in passing through this ideally neat and pretty
village, our tourists must think of the lovely poem of
which all French Canada seems but a reminiscence and
illustration. It was Grand Pré, not Beauport; and they
paid an eager homage to the beautiful genius which has
touched those simple village aspects with an undying
charm, and which, whatever the land's political allegiance, is there perpetual Seigneur.

The village, stretching along the broad intervale of the
St. Lawrence, grows sparser as you draw near the Falls
of Montmorenci, and presently you drive past the grove
shutting from the road the country-house in which the
Duke of Kent spent some merry days of his jovial youth,
and come in sight of two lofty towers of stone,—monuments and witnesses of the tragedy of Montmorenci.

Once a suspension-bridge, built sorely against the will
of the neighbouring *habitans,* hung from these towers

high over the long plunge of the cataract. But one morning of the fatal spring after the first winter's frost had tried the hold of the cable on the rocks, an old peasant and his wife with their little grandson set out in their cart to pass the bridge. As they drew near the middle the anchoring wires suddenly lost their grip upon the shore, and whirled into the air; the bridge crashed under the hapless passengers, and they were launched from its height upon the verge of the Fall, and thence plunged, two hundred and fifty feet, into the ruin of the abyss.

The *habitans* rebuilt their bridge of wood upon low stone piers, so far up the river from the cataract that whoever fell from it would yet have many a chance for life; and it would have been perilous to offer to replace the fallen structure, which, in the belief of faithful Christians, clearly belonged to the numerous bridges built by the Devil, in times when the Devil did not call himself a civil engineer.

The driver, with just unction, recounted the sad tale as he halted his horses on the bridge; and as his passengers looked down the rock-fretted brown torrent towards the Fall, Isabel seized the occasion to shudder that ever she had set foot on that suspension-bridge below Niagara, and to prove to Basil's confusion that her doubt of the bridges between the Three Sisters was not a case of nerves, but an instinctive wisdom concerning the unsafety of all bridges of that design.

From the gate opening into the grounds about the Fall two or three little French boys, whom they had not had the heart to forbid, ran noisily before them with cries in their sole English, "This way, sir!" and led toward a weather-beaten summer-house that tottered upon a projecting rock above the verge of the cataract. But our tourists shook their heads, and turned away for a more distant and less dizzy enjoyment of the spectacle, though any commanding point was sufficiently chasmal and pre-. cipitous. The lofty bluff was scooped inward from the St. Lawrence in a vast irregular semicircle, with cavern-ous hollows, one within another, sinking far into its sides, and naked from foot to crest, or meagrely wooded here and there with evergreen. From the central brink of these gloomy purple chasms the foamy cataract launched itself, and like a cloud,—

"Along the cliff to fall and pause and fall did seem."

I say a cloud, because I find it already said to my hand, as it were, in a pretty verse, and because I must needs liken Montmorenci to something that is soft and light. Yet a cloud does not represent the glinting of the water in its downward swoop; it is like some broad slope of sun-smitten snow; but snow is coldly white and opaque, and this has a creamy warmth in its luminous mass; and so, there hangs the cataract unsaid as before. It is a mystery that anything so grand should be so lovely, that anything so tenderly fair in whatever aspect should yet be so large that one glance fails to comprehend it all. The rugged wildness of the cliffs and hollows about it is soft-ened by its gracious beauty, which half redeems the vul-garity of the timber-merchant's uses in setting the river at work in his saw-mills and choking its outlet into the St. Lawrence with rafts of lumber and rubbish of slabs and shingles. Nay, rather, it is alone amidst these things, and the eye takes note of them by a separate effort.

Our tourists sank down upon the turf that crept with

its white clover to the edge of the precipice, and gazed
dreamily upon the Fall, filling their vision with its exquisite colour and form.   Being wiser than I, they did
not try to utter its loveliness; they were content to feel
it, and the perfection of the afternoon, whose low sun
slanting over the landscape gave, under that pale, green-
ish-blue sky, a pensive sentiment of autumn to the world.
The crickets cried amongst the grass; the hesitating chirp
of birds came from the tree overhead; a shaggy colt left
off grazing in the field and stalked up to stare at them;
their little guides, having found that these people had no
pleasure in the sight of small boys scuffling on the verge
of a precipice, threw themselves also down upon the grass
and crooned a long, long ballad in a mournful minor key
about some maiden whose name was La Belle Adeline.
It was a moment for unmixed enjoyment for every sense,
and through all their being they were glad; which considering, they ceased to be so, with a deep sigh, as one
reasoning that he dreams must presently awake.   They
never could have an emotion without desiring to analyze
it; but perhaps their rapture would have ceased as
swiftly, even if they had not tried to make it a fact of
consciousness.

"If there were not dinner after such experiences as
these," said Isabel, as they sat at table that evening, "I
don't know what would become of one.   But dinner unites
the idea of pleasure and duty, and brings you gently
back to earth.   You *must* eat, don't you see, and there's
nothing disgraceful about what you're obliged to do; and
so—it's all right."

"Isabel, Isabel," cried her husband, "you have a wonderful mind, and its workings always amaze me.   But be

careful, my dear; be careful. Don't work it too hard. The human brain, you know; delicate organ."

"Well, you understand what I mean; and I think it's one of the great charms of a husband, that you're not forced to express yourself to him. A husband," continued Isabel, sententiously, poising a bit of meringue between her thumb and finger,—for they had reached that point in the repast,—"a husband is almost as good as another woman!"

In the parlour they found the Ellisons, and exchanged the history of the day with them.

"Certainly," said Mrs. Ellison, at the end, "it's been a pleasant day enough, but what of the night? You've been turned out, too, by those people who came on the steamer, and who might as well have stayed on board to-night; have you got another room?"

"Not precisely," said Isabel; "we have a coop in the fifth story, right under the roof."

Mrs. Ellison turned energetically upon her husband and cried in tones of reproach, "Richard, Mrs. March has a room!"

"A coop, she *said*," retorted that amiable Colonel, "and we're too good for that. The clerk is keeping us in suspense about a room, because he means to surprise us with something palatial at the end. It's his joking way."

"Nonsense!" said Mrs. Ellison. "Have you seen him since dinner?"

"I have made life a burden to him for the last half-hour," returned the Colonel, with the kindliest smile.

"O Richard," cried his wife, in despair of his amendment, "you wouldn't make life a burden to a mouse!"

And having nothing else for it, she laughed, half in sorrow, half in fondness.

"Well, Fanny," the Colonel irrelevantly answered, "put on your hat and things, and let's all go up to Durham Terrace for a promenade. I know our friends want to go. It's something worth seeing; and by the time we get back, the clerk will have us a perfectly sumptuous apartment."

Nothing, I think, more enforces the illusion of Southern Europe in Quebec than the Sunday-night promenading on Durham Terrace. This is the ample space on the brow of the cliff to the left of the citadel, the noblest and most commanding position in the whole city, which was formerly occupied by the old castle of Saint Louis, where dwelt the brave Count Frontenac and his splendid successors of the French *régime*. The castle went the way of Quebec by fire some forty years ago, and Lord Durham levelled the site and made it a public promenade. A stately arcade of solid masonry supports it on the brink of the rock, and an iron parapet encloses it; there are a few seats to lounge upon, and some idle old guns for the children to clamber over and play with. A soft twilight had followed the day, and there was just enough obscurity to hide from a willing eye the Northern and New World facts of the scene, and to bring into more romantic relief the citadel dark against the mellow evening, and the people gossiping from window to window across the narrow streets of the Lower Town. The Terrace itself was densely thronged, and there was a constant coming and going of the promenaders, who each formally paced back and forth upon the the planking for a certain time, and then went quietly home, giving place to the new arrivals. They were nearly all French, and they were not generally, it seemed, of the first fashion, but rather of middling condition in life; the English being represented only by a few young fellows and now and then a red-faced old gentleman with an Indian scarf trailing from his hat. There were some fair American costumes and faces in the crowd, but it was essentially Quebeckian. The young girls walking in pairs or with their lovers, had the true touch of provincial unstylishness, the young men the ineffectual excess of the second-rate Latin dandy, their elders the rich inelegance of a *bourgeoisie* in their best. A few better-figured *avocats* or *notaires* (their profession was as unmistakeable as if they had carried their well-polished brass door-plates upon their breasts) walked and gravely talked with each other. The non-American character of the scene was not less vividly marked in the fact that each person dressed according to his own taste and frankly indulged private preferences in shapes and colours. One of the promenaders was in white, even to his canvas shoes; another, with yet bolder individuality, appeared in perfect purple. It had a strange, almost portentous effect when these two startling figures met as friends and joined each other in the promenade with linked arms; but the evening was already beginning to darken round them, and presently the purple comrade was merely a sombre shadow beside the glimmering white.

The valleys and the heights now vanished; but the river defined itself by the various coloured lights of the ships and steamers that lay, dark, motionless bulks, upon its broad breast; the lights of Point Levis swarmed upon the other shore; the Lower Town, two hundred feet below them, stretched an alluring mystery of clustering roofs and lamplit windows and dark and shining streets around the mighty rock, mural-crowned. Suddenly a spectacle peculiarly Northern and characteristic of Quebec revealed itself; a long arch brightened over the northern horizon; the tremulous flames of the aurora, pallid violet or faintly tinged with crimson, shot upward from it, and played with a weird apparition and evanescence to the zenith. While the strangers looked, a gun boomed from the citadel, and the wild sweet notes of the bugle sprang out upon the silence.

Then they all said, "How perfectly in keeping everything has been!" and sauntered back to the hotel.

The colonel went into the office to give the clerk another turn on the rack, and make him confess to a hidden apartment somewhere, while Isabel left her husband to Mrs. Ellison in the parlour, and invited Miss Kitty to look at her coop in the fifth story. As they approached, light and music and laughter stole out of an open door next hers, and Isabel, distinguishing the voices of the theatrical party, divined that this was the sick-chamber, and that they were again cheering up the afflicted member of the troupe. Some one was heard to say, "Well, 'ow do you feel now, Charley?" and a sound of subdued swearing responded, followed by more laughter, and the twanging of a guitar, and a snatch of song, and a stir of feet and dresses as for departure.

The two listeners shrank together; as women they could not enjoy these proofs of the jolly *camaraderie* existing among the people of the troupe. They trembled as before the merriment of as many light-hearted, careless good-natured young men; it was no harm, but it was dismaying; and, "Dear!" cried Isabel, "what shall we do?"

"Go back," said Miss Ellison, boldly, and back they ran to the parlour, where they found Basil and the Colonel and his wife in earnest conclave. The Colonel, like a shrewd strategist, was making show of a desperation more violent than his wife's, who was thus naturally forced into the attitude of moderating his fury.

"Well, Fanny, that's all he can do for us; and I do think it's the most outrageous thing in the world! It's real mean!"

Fanny perceived a bold parody of her own denunciatory manner, but just then she was obliged to answer Isabel's eager inquiry whether they had got a room yet. "Yes, *a* room," she said, "with two beds. But what are we to do with one room? That clerk—I don't know what to call him"—("Call him a hotel-clerk, my dear; you can't say anything worse," interrupted her husband)—"seems to think the matter perfectly settled."

"You see, Mrs. March," added the Colonel, "he's able to bully us in this way because he has the architecture on his side. There isn't another room in the house."

"Let me think a moment," said Isabel, not thinking an instant. She had taken a fancy to at least two of these people from the first, and in the last hour they had all become very well acquainted; now she said, "I'll tell you; there are two beds in our room also; we ladies will take one room, and you gentlemen the other!"

"Mrs. March, I bow to the superiority of the Boston mind," said the Colonel, while his females civilly protested and consented; "and I might also hail you as our preserver. If ever you come to Milwaukee,—which is the centre of the world, as Boston is,—we—I—shall be happy to have you call at my place of business.—I didn't commit myself, did I, Fanny?—I am sometimes hospitable to excess, Mrs. March," he said, to explain his aside. "And now, let us reconnoitre. Lead on, madam, and the gratitude of the houseless stranger will follow you."

The whole party explored both rooms, and the ladies decided to keep Isabel's. The Colonel was despatched to see that the wraps and traps of his party were sent to this number, and Basil went with him. The things came long before the gentlemen returned, but the ladies happily employed the interval in talking over the excitements of the day, and in saying from time to time, "So very kind of you, Mrs. March," and "I don't know what we should have done," and "Don't speak of it, please," and "I'm sure it's a great pleasure to me."

In the room adjoining theirs, where the invalid actor lay, and where lately there had been minstrelsy and apparently dancing for his solace, there was now comparative silence. Two women's voices talked together, and now and then a guitar was touched by a wandering hand. Isabel had just put up her handkerchief to conceal her first yawn, when the gentlemen, odorous of cigars, returned to say good-night.

"It's the second door from this, isn't it, Isabel?" asked her husband.

"Yes, the second door. Good-night."

"Good-night."

The two men walked off together; but in a minute afterwards they had returned and were knocking tremulously at the closed door.

"O, what has happened?" chorused the ladies in woful

tune, seeing a certain wildness in the faces that confronted them.

"We don't know!" answered the others in as fearful a key, and related how they had found the door of their room ajar, and a bright light streaming into the corridor. They did not stop to ponder this fact, but, with the heedlessness of their sex, pushed the door wide open, when they saw seated before the mirror a bewildering figure, with dishevelled locks wandering down the back, and in dishabille expressive of being quite at home there, which turned upon them a pair of blue eyes, under a forehead remarkable for the straggling fringe of hair that covered it. They professed to have remained transfixed at the sight, and to have noted a like dismay on the visage before the glass, ere they summoned strength to fly. These facts Colonel Ellison gave at the command of his wife, with many protests and insincere delays amidst which the curiosity of his hearers alone prevented them from rending him in pieces.

"And what do you suppose it was?" demanded his wife, with forced calmness, when he had at last made an end of the story and his abominable hypocrisies.

"Well, *I* think it was a mermaid."

"A mermaid!" said his wife, scornfully. "How do you know?"

"It had a comb in its hand, for one thing; and besides, my dear, I hope I know a mermaid when I see it."

"Well," said Mrs. Ellison, "it was no mermaid, it was a mistake; and I'm going to see about it. Will you go with me, Richard?"

"No money could induce me! If it's a mistake, it isn't proper for me to go; if it's a mermaid, it's dangerous."

"O you coward!" said the intrepid little woman to a hero of all the fights on Sherman's march to the sea; and presently they heard her attack the mysterious enemy with a ladylike courage, claiming the invaded chamber. The foe replied with like civility, saying the clerk had given her that room with the understanding that another lady was to be put there with her, and she had left the door unlocked to admit her. The watchers with the sick man next door appeared and confirmed this speech; a feeble voice from the bed-clothes swore to it.

"Of course," added the invader, "if I'd known 'ow it really was, I never would 'ave listened to such a thing, never. And there isn't another 'ole in the 'ouse to lay me 'ead, she concluded.

"Then it's the clerk's fault," said Mrs. Ellison, glad to retreat unharmed; and she made her husband ring for the guilty wretch, a pale, quiet young Frenchman, whom the united party, sallying into the corridor, began to upbraid in one breath, the lady in dishabille vanishing as often as she remembered it, and reappearing whenever some strong point of argument or denunciation occurred to her.

The clerk, who was the Benjamin of his wicked tribe, threw himself upon their mercy and confessed everything: the house was so crowded, and he had been so crazed by the demands upon him, that he had understood Colonel Ellison's application to be for a bed for the young lady in his party, and he had done the very best he could. If the lady there—she vanished again—would give up the room to the two gentlemen, he would find her a place with the housekeeper. To this the lady consented without difficulty, and the rest dispersing, she kissed one of the sick man's watchers with "Isn't it a shame, Bella?" and flitted down the darkness of the corridor. The rooms upon it seemed all, save the two assigned our travellers, to be occupied by ladies of the troupe; their doors successively opened, and she was heard explaining to each as she passed. The momentary displeasure which she had shown at her banishment was over. She detailed the facts with perfect good-nature, and though the others appeared no more than herself to find any humorous cast in the affair, they received her narration with the same amiability. They uttered their sympathy seriously, and each parted from her with some friendly word. Then all was still.

"Richard," said Mrs. Ellison, when in Isabel's room the travellers had briefly celebrated these events, "I should think you'd hate to leave us alone up here."

"I do; but you can't think how I hate to go off alone. I wish you'd come part of the way with us, ladies; I do indeed. Leave your door unlocked, at any rate."

This prayer, uttered at parting outside the room, was answered from within by a sound of turning keys and sliding bolts, and a low thunder as of bureaus and wash-stands rolled against the door. "The ladies are fortifying their position," said the Colonel to Basil, and the two returned to their own chamber. "I don't wish any intrusions," he said, instantly shutting himself in; "my nerves are too much shaken now. What an awfully mysterious old place this Quebec is, Mr. March! I'll tell you what: it's my opinion that this is an enchanted castle, and if my ribs are not walked over by a muleteer in the course of the night, it's all I ask."

In this and other discourse recalling the famous ad-

o

venture of Don Quixote, the Colonel beguiled the labour of disrobing, and had got as far as his boots, when there came a startling knock at the door. With one boot in his hand and the other on his foot, the Colonel limped forward. "I suppose it's that clerk has sent to say he's made some other mistake," and he flung wide the door, and then stood motionless before it, humbly staring at a figure on the threshold,—a figure with the fringed forehead and pale blue eyes of her whom they had so lately turned out of that room.

Shrinking behind the side of the doorway, "Excuse me, gentlemen," she said, with a dignity that recalled their scattered senses, "but will you 'ave the goodness to look if my beads are on your table? O thanks, thanks, thanks!" she continued, showing her face and one hand, as Basil blushingly advanced with a string of heavy black beads, piously adorned with a large cross. "I'm sure, I'm greatly obliged to you, gentlemen, and I hask a thousand pardons for troublin' you," she concluded in a somewhat severe tone, that left them abashed and culpable; and vanished as mysteriously as she had appeared.

"Now, see here," said the Colonel, with a huge sigh as he closed the door again, and this time locked it, "I should like to know how long this sort of thing is to be kept up? Because, if it's to be regularly repeated during the night, I'm going to dress again." Nevertheless, he finished undressing and got into bed, where he remained for some time silent. Basil put out the light. "O, I'm sorry you did that, my dear fellow," said the Colonel; "but never mind, it was an idle curiosity, no doubt. It's my belief that in the landlord's extremity of bed-linen, I've been put to sleep between a pair of table-

cloths; and I thought I'd like to look. It seems to me
that I make out a checkered pattern on top and a flowered
or arabesque pattern underneath. I wish they had given
me mates. It's pretty hard having to sleep between odd
table-cloths. I shall complain to the landlord of this in
the morning. I've never had to sleep between *odd* table-
cloths at *any* hotel before."

The Colonel's voice seemed scarcely to have died away
upon Basil's drowsy ear, when suddenly the sounds of
music and laughter from the invalid's room startled him
wide awake. The sick man's watchers were coquetting
with some one who stood in the little courtyard five
stories below. A certain breadth of repartee was naturally allowable at that distance; the lover avowed his passion in ardent terms, and the ladies mocked him with the
same freedom, now and then totally neglecting him while
they sang a snatch of song to the twanging of the guitar,
or talked professional gossip, and then returning to him
with some tormenting expression of tenderness.

All this, abstractly speaking, was nothing to Basil;
yet he could recollect few things intended for his pleasure that had given him more satisfaction. He thought,
as he glanced out into the moonlight on the high-gabled
silvery roofs around and on the gardens of the convents
and the towers of the quaint city, that the scene wanted
nothing of the proper charm of Spanish humour and romance, and he was as grateful to those poor souls as if
they had meant him a favour. To us of the hither side
of the foot-lights, there is always something fascinating
in the life of the strange beings who dwell beyond them,
and who are never so unreal as in their own characters.
In their shabby bestowal in those mean upper rooms,

their tawdry poverty, their merry submission to the errors and caprices of destiny, their mutual kindliness and careless friendship, these unprofitable devotees of the twinkling-footed burlesque seemed to be playing rather than living the life of strolling players; and their love-making was the last touch of a comedy that Basil could hardly accept as reality, it was so much more like something seen upon the stage. He would not have detracted anything from the commonness and cheapness of the *mise en scène*, for that, he reflected drowsily and confusedly, helped to give it an air of fact and make it like an episode of fiction. But above all, he was pleased with the natural eventlessness of the whole adventure, which was in perfect agreement with his taste; and just as his reveries began to lose shape in dreams, he was aware of an absurd pride in the fact that all this could have happened to him in our commonplace time and hemisphere. "Why," he thought, "if I were a student in Alcalá, what better could I have asked?" And as at last his soul swung out from its moorings and lapsed down the broad slowly circling tides out in the sea of sleep, he was conscious of one subtle touch of compassion for those poor strollers,—a pity so delicate and fine and tender that it hardly seemed his own, but rather a sense of the compassion that pities the whole world.

X.

HOMEWARD AND HOME

THE travellers all met at breakfast and duly discussed the adventures of the night; and for the rest, the forenoon passed rapidly and slowly with Basil and Isabel, as regret to leave Quebec, or the natural impatience of travellers to be off, overcame them. Isabel spent part of it in shopping, for she had found some small sums of money and certain odd corners in her trunks still unappropriated, and the handsome stores on the Rue Fabrique were very tempting. She said she would just go in and look; and the wise reader imagines the result. As she knelt over her boxes, trying so to distribute her purchases as to make them look as if they were old,—old things of hers, which she had brought all the way round from Boston with her,—a fleeting touch of conscience stayed her hand.

"Basil," she said, "perhaps we'd better declare *some* of these things. What's the duty on those?" she asked, pointing to certain articles.

"I don't know. About a hundred per cent. *ad valorem.*

"*C'est à dire—?*"

"As much as they cost."

"O *then,* dearest," responded Isabel indignantly, "it *can't* be wrong to smuggle! I won't declare a thread!"

"That's very well for you, whom they won't ask. But what if they ask *me* whether there's anything to declare?"

Isabel looked at her husband and hesitated. Then she replied in terms that I am proud to record in honour of American womanhood: "You mustn't fib about it, Basil" (heroically); "I couldn't respect you if you did" (tenderly); "but" (with decision) *"you must slip out of it some way!"*

The ladies of the Ellison party, to whom she put the case in the parlour, agreed with her perfectly. They also had done a little shopping in Quebec, and they meant to do more at Montreal before they returned to the States. Mrs. Ellison was disposed to look upon Isabel's compunctions as a kind of treason to the sex, to be forgiven only because so quickly repented.

The Ellisons were going up the Saguenay before coming on to Boston, and urged our friends hard to go with them. "No, that must be for another time," said Isabel. "Mr. March has to be home by a certain day; and we shall just get back in season." Then she made them promise to spend a day with her in Boston, and the Colonel coming to say that he had a carriage at the door for their excursion to Lorette, the two parties bade good-bye with affection and many explicit hopes of meeting soon again.

"What do you think of them, dearest?" demanded Isabel, as she sallied out with Basil for a final look at Quebec.

"The young lady is the nicest; and the other is well enough, too. She is a good deal like you, but with the sense of humour left out. You've only enough to save you."

"Well, her husband is jolly enough for both of them. He's funnier than you, Basil, and he hasn't any of your little languid airs and affectations. I don't know but I'm a bit disappointed in my choice, darling; but I daresay I shall work out of it. In fact, I don't know but the Colonel is a little *too* jolly. This drolling everything is rather fatiguing." And having begun, they did not stop till they had taken their friends to pieces. Dismayed, then, they hastily reconstructed them, and said that they were among the pleasantest people they ever knew, and they were really very sorry to part with them, and they should do everything to make them have a good time in Boston.

They were sauntering towards Durham Terrace, where they leaned long upon the iron parapet and blest themselves with the beauty of the prospect. A tender haze hung upon the landscape and subdued it till the scene was as a dream before them. As in a dream the river lay, and dream-like the shipping moved or rested on its deep, broad bosom. Far off stretched the happy fields with their dim white villages; further still the mellow heights melted into the low hovering heaven. The tinned roofs of the Lower Town twinkled in the morning sun; around them on every hand, on that Monday forenoon when the States were stirring from ocean to ocean in feverish industry, drowsed the grey city within her walls; from the flag-staff of the citadel hung the red banner of Saint George in sleep.

Their hearts were strangely and deeply moved. It seemed to them that they looked upon the last stronghold of the Past, and that afar off to the southward they could hear the marching hosts of the invading Present; and as no young and loving soul can relinquish old things without a pang, they sighed a long mute farewell to Quebec.

Next summer they would come again, yes; but, ah me! every one knows what next summer is!

Part of the burlesque troupe rode down in the omnibus to the Grand Trunk Ferry with them, and were good-natured to the last, having shaken hands all round with the waiters, chambermaids, and porters of the hotel. The young fellow with the bad amiable face came in a calash, and refused to over-pay the driver with a gay decision that made him Basil's envy till he saw his tribu-lation in getting the troupe's luggage checked. There were forty pieces, and it always remained a mystery, considering the small amount of clothing necessary to those people on the stage, what could have filled their trunks. The young man and the two English blondes of American birth found places in the same car with our tourists, and enlivened the journey with their frolics. When the young man pretended to fall asleep, they wrapped his golden curly head in a shawl, and vexed him with many thumps and thrusts, till he bought a brief truce with a handful of almonds; and the ladies having no other way to eat them, one of them saucily snatched off her shoe, and cracked them hammerwise with the heel. It was all so pleasant that it ought to have been all right; and in their merry world of outlawry perhaps things are not so bad as we like to think them.

The country into which the train plunges as soon as Quebec is out of sight is very stupidly savage, and our friends had little else to do but watch the gambols of the players, till they came to the river St. Francis, whose wandering loveliness the road follows through an infinite series of soft and beautiful landscapes, and find every-where glassing in its smooth current the elms and willows